I0759986

A Year of Ikigai

Finding Everyday Purpose Through Japanese Wisdom

NICHOLAS KEMP
FOUNDER OF IKIGAI TRIBE

ROCK POINT

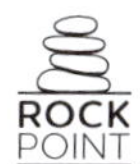

With gratitude to the people
of Japan—from strangers to family
and friends—whose kindness, wisdom,
and spirit have given me
the gift of ikigai.

Contents

Introduction: What Is Ikigai? 6

How to Read This Book 10

IKIGAI MYTHS 12

UNDERSTANDING IKIGAI 18

GAI 34

MIEKO KAMIYA 40

THE CHARACTERISTICS OF IKIGAI 46

IKIGAI VALUES 52

IKIGAI SOURCES 57

THE IKIGAI-9 SCALE 63

WHERE IKIGAI IS FOUND 69

LEISURE 79

GROWTH 82

A BRIGHT FUTURE 85

RESONANCE 88

FREEDOM 91

SELF-ACTUALIZATION 94

MEANING AND VALUE 97

PURPOSE 100

ENERGY 103
FLOW 106
IKIGAI AND YOUR KOKORO 109
NATURE 112
KOTODAMA 118
HAIKU 124
DŌ—THE PATH, THE WAY 127
CHANOYU 130
IKIGAI ASKS YOU TO 133
IKIGAI STORIES 138
ACTIVATE YOUR IKIGAI 188
SLOW DOWN TO FEEL IKIGAI 198
RETURN IKIGAI TO OTHERS 204
CONTINUE YOUR IKIGAI JOURNALING 210
Conclusion: Make Life Worth Living 215
List of Quotees 219
References 220
Acknowledgments 222
About the Author 223

Introduction

What Is Ikigai?

The fact that you're alive to read these words is nothing short of a miracle. Thousands upon thousands of generations in your ancestral chain all lived long enough, met, and procreated at the exact right time to eventually produce you. In short, you and I won the jackpot in the evolutionary lottery. Yet, we don't treat life as a miracle. Most of the time, we struggle to get through each day. The Japanese concept of ikigai reminds us that life is a miracle—a patchwork of small wonders and special moments, once-in-a-lifetime experiences and life-changing opportunities we can embrace, nurture, and appreciate if we choose to do so. In short, having ikigai makes life feel worth living.

For close to a decade, the West has had a fascination with ikigai, with many people believing that it is a concept from Okinawa, the secret to living a long and happy life, and a sweet spot where you find your dream job or bliss in life. Best-selling books, numerous TED Talks, thousands of blog articles, and endless social media posts perpetuate and continue to promote false notions of what ikigai is and what motivates Japanese people to get out of bed in the morning.

Unfortunately, many common Western thoughts are nothing more than romanticized interpretations that have misled millions of people into believing that ikigai originates from a "blue zone," a part of the world that has a high concentration of centenarians.

Another false interpretation is that ikigai must be something you love, you are good at, that serves the world, and that can be paid for in order for you to experience it.

The truth is, ikigai encompasses all aspects of one's life with an emphasis on the intrinsic elements that provide a sense of meaning and fulfillment. Ikigai includes life-affirming facets we might relate to positive psychology, such as life satisfaction, growth, hope, social affiliation, freedom, self-actualization, meaning, and purpose.

A closer look at the word—and its kanji, 生き甲斐—helps us understand ikigai's meaning and application. *Ikigai* is a compound of two terms: *iki* (from the verb *ikiru* 生きる), meaning "to live," and *gai*, (甲斐), meaning "value" or "worth." In a nutshell, ikigai is what you live for—what makes your existence meaningful.

If we take a closer look at the kanji of the suffix *kai* (甲斐) it leads us to a deeper level of understanding. The first character, 甲, means "armor" or "shell," suggesting that ikigai includes the things that protect you or help you cope with life. The second character, 斐, indicates something "beautiful" and "patterned," much like how life is a tapestry. Together, these two kanji suggest that ikigai encompasses both the things that help you endure life's challenges and enjoy the beautiful moments, and experiences that make life feel worth living.

Here, it is crucial to understand what we mean by "life." We are not referring to your life in the broad, existential sense—ikigai is rooted in daily existence, in the small, meaningful moments that shape everyday life. Ikigai is not made of grand plans or embracing an all-or-nothing attitude. Ikigai is what you make of your everyday.

Note: Kai (甲斐) becomes gai in ikigai due to rendaku, a common sound change in Japanese where the first consonant of the second word in a compound is voiced. Also, gai in ikigai is usually written in hiragana, the basic Japanese syllabary (生きがい) to give the word a softer, more approachable feel.

Despite the growing popularity of ikigai in the West, the irony is that most Japanese rarely use the word or consciously think about the concept in daily life. For Japanese people, ikigai is something they feel rather than talk about. If they do discuss it, it's often in a casual way, much like they would speak about their hobbies. Ikigai isn't a grand life philosophy or a structured framework—it's simply something that brings joy and a small lift to life. Ultimately, ikigai is personal and unique to each individual. For a new parent, it may be their child. For an entrepreneur, it may be their work. And for an alcoholic, it may be booze. There's no universal "right" or "wrong" ikigai, but it can be deeply life-affirming.

Ikigai entered my life more than twenty-five years ago, in 1998, through a casual conversation I had with a Japanese coworker on the first day of a job in Tokyo. My coworker's explanation of ikigai filled me with excitement and left me intrigued. I couldn't believe the Japanese language had a single word that encapsulated what makes life worth living and the reasons we battle on through life. That conversation stuck with me, even as life moved on.

Twenty years later, I encountered the word again in the center of a four-circle Venn diagram with the following questions: Are you doing something that you love? Are you doing something that you're good at? Are you doing something that the world needs? Are you doing something that you can be paid for? In the center, where all four circles overlap, was the word *ikigai*.

It is believed and perpetuated by many Westerners/non-Japanese that as ikigai lies at the center of these interconnecting circles, if you are lacking in one or more of these areas (e.g., you are doing something that you love and are good at, but are not serving the world or making money from it), then you can't experience ikigai and are therefore missing out on living a meaningful and fulfilling life. This is obviously not the case.

I started seeing the word ikigai and this Venn diagram more and more online. It was everywhere: on social media, in blog posts, and on TED talks.

Then one day, I was shocked to discover the Venn diagram as the ikigai concept on the World Economic Forum website. It felt like a clear case of cultural appropriation—an oversimplified, Westernized version of a deeply Japanese concept being presented as universal truth. And yes, I'm fully aware of the irony here: I'm a non-Japanese Westerner writing a book about ikigai. But that's exactly why I felt compelled to dig deeper. I didn't want to add to the noise—I wanted to understand the real meaning of ikigai from those who live it. That was the spark that started my journey, and a podcast, to uncover the mystery behind the Venn diagram and the truth about ikigai.

Six years on, and the journey to understanding ikigai has dramatically changed my life. For one, I'm writing this book. Through my podcast, *The Ikigai Podcast*, which explores ikigai from the perspective of the Japanese, I have connected with many inspiring Japanese academics, researchers, artists, tea masters, Shinto priests and Zen monks, as well as everyday people who were willing to share their ikigai. The podcast led to me establishing a coach training business and building a community of inspiring coaches and educators I call Ikigai Tribe. More recently, ikigai has brought me back to Japan, and I now take business leaders, coaches, and entrepreneurs on ikigai retreats—Japanese cultural study trips where guests can experience ikigai in Japan with locals through cultural practices and traditional craft.

According to Japan's research pioneer, Mieko Kamiya, whom I like to call the Mother of Ikigai, the word *ikigai* refers to the sources of value in one's life—the things that make one's life worthwhile. These sources could include people, roles, relationships, work, hobbies, goals, dreams, and even memories. The life-affirming feelings that arise from these sources—the deep awareness that life is worth living—are called *ikigai-kan*, with *kan* meaning "sense, perception, awareness of feeling."

In short, ikigai is what makes life *feel* worth living.

How to Read This Book

To get the most out of this journey, I recommend reading the book in order. It's carefully structured to guide you step-by-step: first introducing ikigai, then helping you understand how it's viewed in Japan, showing you ways to find it in the world around you, and finally helping you activate and live it in your own life.

Take your time. Read slowly. Let each daily entry be a gentle invitation to pause and reflect. You'll find journal prompts, reflections, and small activities throughout the book—all meant to inspire you to uncover and embrace your ikigai.

Finding your ikigai means getting to know yourself deeply and exploring what truly matters to you. Your ikigai is unique to you—it's what makes life feel meaningful and fulfilling. That could come from your past, your present moments, or your hopes for the future. I recommend keeping a journal as you read to help capture those insights and answer the prompts throughout.

Seeking the truth about ikigai has been a personal quest for me. I imagine it's important to you, too—and that's why you're here. My goal is to show that ikigai touches every part of life, with a focus on the inner elements that give our existence depth and purpose. To help bring this idea to light, I've included stories and reflections from Japanese people of all ages and backgrounds—from school children and university students to ikigai researchers and Zen priests.

I hope *A Year of Ikigai* becomes a meaningful companion as you explore your own purpose, and that it brings you clarity, joy, and a deeper sense of fulfillment each day.

生きがいの神話 Ikigai Myths

DAY 1 • IKIGAI—JAPAN'S MOST MISUNDERSTOOD WORD

As we begin this ikigai journey together, I invite you to let go of what you know about ikigai and start with a beginner's mind, opening yourself up to all the possibilities ikigai has to offer. As we'll discover in this chapter, much of what is shared about ikigai outside of Japan is factually incorrect. If you can let go of your preconceived notions, our journey together will be far more insightful, fulfilling, and rewarding. I also encourage you to start writing down any insights in your journal today to keep track of your growth. So, let's bust these myths and start our journey on the right foot.

DAY 2 • THE IKIGAI VENN DIAGRAM

If you search the term *ikigai* on Google, you will inevitably come across a four-circle Venn diagram with the following questions: Are you doing something that you love? Are you doing something that you're good at? Are you doing something that the world needs? Are you doing something that you can be paid for? In the center, where all four circles overlap, is the word *ikigai*, implying that true ikigai exists only when all four of these conditions are met. While inspiring and seductive, boxing ikigai into a sweet spot is just plain wrong and limits its life-affirming potential. What parts of your life feel meaningful to you—even if they don't fit into this Venn diagram?

DAY 3 • IKIGAI AS A SWEET SPOT

Rather than a sweet spot, ikigai is a spectrum of the life-affirming aspects of your existence. This can include your roles and relationships, hobbies, aspects of your work, goals and ambitions, and even memories. Ikigai is not something to achieve; it's what you feel makes your life worth living. The concept is subjective and personal. Over the next four days, we'll take a look at why the four questions of the Venn diagram don't add up to define ikigai. First, make a quick list of all the things in your life that make you feel life is worth living. Don't think too much; this is just to get you heartstorming.

DAY 4 • IKIGAI IS SOMETHING YOU LOVE

Ikigai can definitely include something you love. More specifically, ikigai is often something that you love doing, such as pursuing a hobby you are passionate about or engaging in work that you find purposeful and rewarding. But ikigai is not just limited to something you love; it is often someone you love—your partner, your friends, or your children. I would also like to point out that ikigai can include overcoming adversity, taking on challenges, or even engaging in unpleasant activities that will help you uncover your potential. What challenges have made you the person you are today? And whom do you love?

DAY 5 • IKIGAI IS SOMETHING THAT YOU ARE GOOD AT

Ikigai can be something that you are good at, but being overzealous in this belief limits your ikigai to what you currently excel at. Ikigai is more about something that you want to become good at, as the concept is tied to growth and involves learning and trying new things. Ikigai can also be something you are bad at. If you are a bad singer but love singing, then that could be your ikigai. If it makes your life feel worth living, keep doing it regardless of how well you can do it.

DAY 6 • IKIGAI IS SOMETHING THE WORLD NEEDS

Ikigai is not something the world needs; it's something you need. It's what you need to make your life worth living. It's what you need to make life meaningful to you. It's what you need to help you get through the day or week. It's what you need to help you put up with life's hassles. Ikigai can include serving others or working toward a goal that benefits society, but because ikigai is something deeply personal, more often than not, it is something you do for yourself.

DAY 7 • IKIGAI IS SOMETHING THAT YOU ARE PAID FOR

Ikigai is definitely not something you need to be paid for to experience. In fact, the opposite is true; ikigai is often something you'd happily pay to do or experience. Ikigai does not involve the accumulation of money. If you need to be paid to feel a sense of ikigai, then that's not ikigai. Ikigai is something you do or engage in simply because doing so makes you feel alive. In short, ikigai is something that is intrinsically motivating.

DAY 8 • IKIGAI IS A WORD AND CONCEPT FROM OKINAWA

Ikigai is believed by many to originate from Okinawa, a "blue zone," one of the places in the world that has a high concentration of centenarians. Consequently, Westerners have had a tendency to inappropriately connect ikigai to the longevity of Okinawans. The reality is that ikigai is a common word in the Japanese language, and not a word they relate to longevity. How has the Western interpretation shaped your understanding of ikigai? How might you explore its meaning in a more personal and authentic way?

DAY 9 • IKIGAI IS THE SECRET TO LONGEVITY

While ikigai can give you the motivation to live, it can't guarantee that you'll live to be one hundred. People with ikigai are likely to engage in self-care behaviors, improving their chances of living longer. However, if your ikigai is overindulging in food and alcohol, your chances of living a long life are reduced. Ikigai is diminished if we merely think of it as the secret to longevity, but a life worth living is one we should try to sustain for as long as possible. Are your sources of fulfillment supporting your well-being, or are there habits that might need adjusting?

DAY 10 • HAVING IKIGAI MEANS YOU NEVER RETIRE

Japanese people most certainly retire. And for many Japanese, ikigai is something they explore, uncover, and pursue after retirement, when they have the time and financial stability to do so. In fact, since the 1980s, there have been many government initiatives to help Japanese retirees do so. One such example is Japan's Health-Ikigai Creation Advisors, who help retirees transition from a work role to a social role. With Japan's notorious work culture—long working hours, workplace abuse, and few holidays—never retiring would definitely make some lives not worth living. What makes your life worth living outside of work? What plans do you have for life after retirement?

生きがいとは Understanding Ikigai

DAY 11 • IKIGAI IS WHAT MATTERS

Who and what matters to you today? If you can answer this question, then you have uncovered your ikigai, at least for the present moment. What matters to you will change as the circumstances of your life change. Some sources of ikigai will remain constant in your life, while others will come and go. As a lived experience, ikigai is both enduring and ephemeral. What's important is to appreciate it in the now. What matters to you right now? Go and do it. Who matters to you right now? Spend time with them.

DAY 12 • IKIGAI IS EXPERIENTIAL

Ikigai is experiential by nature; that is to say, you experience it. It is not a theory. It is something lived. It comes with emotions and physical sensations. You feel it. Your ikigai is shaped by your experiences of the past, what currently matters to you, and what you hope to experience in the future. The more experiences you have in life, the more you understand ikigai. If a life well-lived is full of ikigai, then it is a life that comes with many experiences. What past experiences have made you feel life is worth living?

DAY 13 • IKIGAI IS EMOTIONAL

Ikigai is felt, often physically, but more specifically emotionally. Your emotions confirm your ikigai sources. When you are emotional, that's ikigai talking to you, telling you what matters and what you care about. The deeper you feel toward someone or something, the stronger the ikigai source that emotion is tied to. As with all things in life, ikigai comes with mixed emotions—joy, sadness, vulnerability. What emotions tell you life is worth living?

DAY 14 • IKIGAI IS PSYCHOLOGICAL

Ikigai is Japan's unique measure of well-being, which we could relate to positive psychology. Many psychometric tools measure ikigai in the domains of purpose, meaning, life satisfaction, sense of freedom, personal growth, and self-actualization. As ikigai is of the mind, related to how we interpret, understand, feel, and make meaning of what is positive, it is psychological. In short, we can understand ikigai as the psychological condition of flourishing. When you feel ikigai you are flourishing. What makes you flourish?

DAY 15 • IKIGAI IS PHILOSOPHICAL

Ikigai is the Japanese lens for how to understand life, inviting you to think deeply about your internal world and the world around you. It involves making meaning of life's experiences and making sense of life's most fundamental human questions: *What am I living for? What gives my life meaning? What should I do with my life?* From time to time, we all ask ourselves such questions. Ikigai gives you the space and experiences to find your answers. What currently gives purpose to your life?

DAY 16 • IKIGAI IS EXISTENTIAL

In an existential context, ikigai asks the question: What makes life worth continuing? An existential crisis often follows a loss of ikigai. This reveals why it is crucial to have many sources of ikigai in your life. Ikigai isn't a single role, relationship, or belief to stake your whole life on. It is a spectrum—a rich collection of the people, passions, and small joys that make life worth living. What people, passions, and small joys in your spectrum of ikigai help you get through your toughest days?

DAY 17 • IKIGAI IS LOGICAL

Ikigai is logical—not in the sense that one plus one equals two, but in an inner personal sense. It helps you make decisions that align with your values and strengths. When you know what your ikigai includes, it becomes easier for you to make important life decisions. For example, leaving a high-paying secure job to open a patisserie might seem irrational to others, but if baking cakes and pastries is what you love doing, then the decision would be logical *to you*. Your inner logic helps you make *ikigai decisions* that make sense to you and bring more meaning into your life. What's an ikigai decision—a life changing and life affirming decision—you'd like to make?

DAY 18 • IKIGAI IS RELATIONAL

Ikigai is best experienced with others. It's often not what you do, but who you do it with. Ikigai are those shared life moments where you feel warmth by simply being together with someone you love, find meaning in a conversation with a friend, or experience a sense of purpose in a task you would struggle to do alone. In short, ikigai is social intelligence at play, telling you who to share your life with. Who do you want to spend your time with?

DAY 19 • IKIGAI IS SOCIAL

Ikigai helps you answer the question: *What's my place in society*? It acts like social glue, strongly connecting you to others in your various communities. It guides you toward what roles to take on and how to fulfill them. These are the roles that serve a greater good and come with a sense of purpose. Having such roles gives you meaning and a strong sense of identity, while also building your self-esteem. If you feel needed and believe that what you contribute to society matters, your ikigai is flourishing. Where and by whom do you feel needed?

DAY 20 • IKIGAI IS SPIRITUAL

While ikigai doesn't belong to any specific religion, it is spiritual in that it can create inner peace for you and connect you to something greater than yourself. For some, ikigai is their relationship with God, the divine, or a higher power, as it provides hope and meaning to their life. For others, it's their connection with their inner spirit, giving them clarity on how to live their life. Ultimately, ikigai frees your spirit to express itself. What is your spirit telling you to do?

DAY 21 • IKIGAI IS PERSONAL

Ikigai is ultimately personal. It's what gives your life meaning. It's what gives your life purpose. It's actually what makes you *you*. It changes and grows as you do. You are your own ikigai source, and if you can accept and respect yourself, you'll enjoy life a lot more. Ikigai frees you to be you, to do what you want and to express yourself in ways that are true to who you are. When do you feel most like yourself?

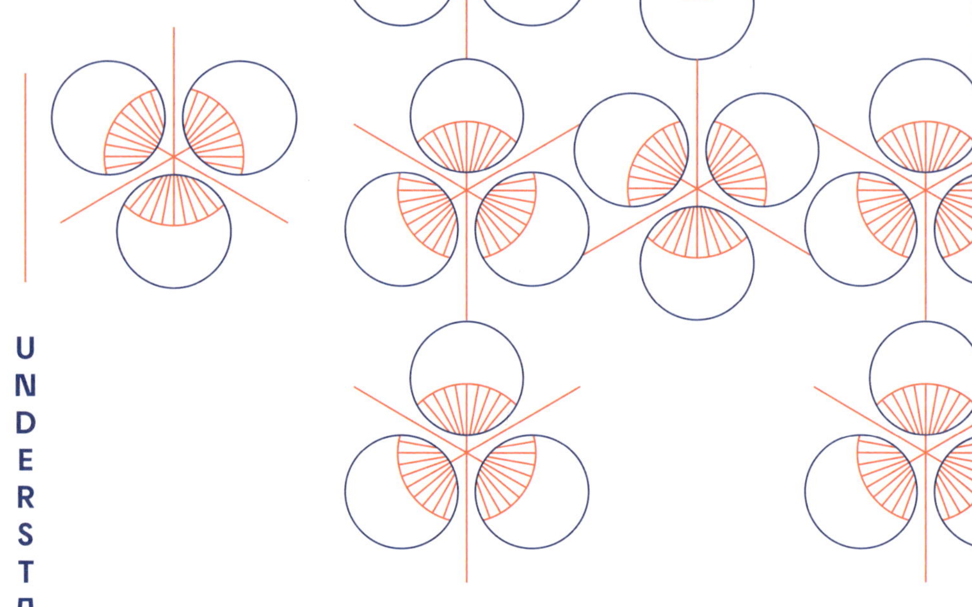

DAY 22 • IKIGAI IS INTUITIVE

Ikigai is what feels right for you, something that naturally comes to you. There are no rules or formulas when it comes to ikigai. We want to avoid Venn diagrams and step-by-step instructions to find it. Instead, notice and listen to your intuition when it taps you on the shoulder. Your first encounter with a new ikigai source will come with an inner knowing that it fits for you. What has your intuition revealed to you recently?

DAY 23 • IKIGAI IS SUBJECTIVE

Ikigai is purely subjective. It's what you find personally meaningful and life-affirming. Like you and your personality, your ikigai sources are unique. And while some sources of ikigai can be shared, they are experienced and felt differently by each person. Just as you grow and change, so too will your ikigai. As your view on what matters in life shifts, new sources of ikigai will emerge. What's one source of ikigai that feels especially unique to you? It could be something quirky or even embarrassing.

DAY 24 • IKIGAI IS TEMPORAL

Ikigai is shaped by your past, lived in the present, and directed toward the future. It flows with your life, adjusting to your changing needs, desires, and circumstances. This makes ikigai dynamic: responsive to change, yet impermanent, even fleeting. Your ikigai sources twenty years from now will likely be very different from those you enjoy today. There are also ikigai moments that only happen once, never to be experienced again. In the context of time, ikigai asks three essential questions: What have you learned from your past? What matters to you now? What do you want for your future?

DAY 25 • IKIGAI IS REFLECTIVE

Ikigai encourages you to look back and explore what you can learn from your past. Our past shapes who we are; the more we reflect on it, the more we understand ourselves and what matters to us. This helps us better understand what we want out of life.

Being reflective also gives you a chance to reconnect with the ikigai sources of your past, some of which you may wish to rekindle and bring into the present. What's a past ikigai source you gave up that you'd like to rekindle?

DAY 26 • IKIGAI IS CONTEMPLATIVE

Ikigai asks you to look within and reflect on life's bigger questions to make meaning of your existence. When you are deep in thought, trying to make sense of your present life, that's ikigai having a conversation with you: asking you what matters and poking you about how you want to live your life. It's important for you and your ikigai to create the space to do this. Inner dialogue is often triggered by the loss of a role or the end of a relationship, but being contemplative should be a daily practice. What questions would you like to make space for?

DAY 27 • IKIGAI IS INTRINSIC

Ikigai includes the things you feel like doing simply because they make you feel alive. It's something you can't wait to start and might stay up late doing for hours. It's often an activity that will put you in a flow state—where you are so deeply engaged that you forget to eat and lose track of time. That's ikigai, alive and kicking. Ikigai doesn't require recognition or reward. The reward of ikigai is the source itself. What's something you'd eagerly seek out—not for gain, but for the sheer joy of doing it?

DAY 28 • IKIGAI IS LIFE-AFFIRMING

Ikigai affirms your life. It's what makes you want to keep on living. Identifying the contributors—the people, relationships, roles, activities, experiences, and so on—that make you feel this way is the key to maximizing your ikigai. You need to know what makes your life worth living so you can nurture it. Ikigai doesn't involve making life affirmations or trying to will something into your life. It's what you can recognize that already makes your life meaningful. What can you identify right now that affirms your life?

DAY 29 • IKIGAI IS HOLISTIC

Ikigai involves all aspects of your human experience—you think it, feel it, and embody it. If ikigai has a goal, then it is for you to live life fully and holistically. Ikigai is not the pursuit of a single experience in life; it is the whole experience of life. This is why the West's interpretation of ikigai, the alluring sweet spot of that four-circle Venn diagram, is so off the mark. Ikigai goes far beyond a dream job. What areas of your life require more attention?

DAY 30 • IKIGAI STARTS WITH YOUR VALUES

Ikigai emerges when you live in harmony with your values—not those that you have inherited or been pressured to accept by outside influences, but those that you have identified for yourself. If you live in conflict or are forced to compromise your values, then ikigai will remain elusive. Create a list of your values. Are there areas in your daily life where you feel disconnected from them? Once you have clarity on your values, take one small step to align your daily actions with them.

DAY 31 • IKIGAI GUIDES YOU

As ikigai is built on your values and what you hold dear, it guides you to make the right choices and life decisions. It's your inner compass helping you stay on the path of a life well lived. When you find yourself feeling afraid or anxious, connect with ikigai by slowing down to ask yourself what really matters. Doing so will give you the clarity to move forward. Are you struggling with a choice or important decision at the moment? Ask yourself: *Will choosing this option bring more ikigai into my life?*

DAY 32 • IKIGAI GROUNDS YOU

Ikigai keeps you grounded when life gets overwhelming and you feel things are about to spiral out of control. Ikigai includes the little rituals, habits, or even chores that help you slow down and keep you focused and present. Ikigai also helps keep your ego in check, reminding you to be authentic, humble, and honest when luck or opportunity finds its way to you. What helps you stay grounded?

DAY 33 • IKIGAI COMFORTS YOU

Ikigai gives you comfort when life becomes a struggle. It could be comfort food, a warm drink, soothing music, or a heart-to-heart conversation with a friend you trust. When you are dealing with loss or uncertainty, or are just down on your luck, ikigai acts as a healthy coping mechanism, giving you the space and time to breathe a little easier. What are the things you turn to when life is hard? Write a list of the things that comfort you and reflect on why they help you in times of need.

DAY 34 • IKIGAI EXCITES YOU

Ikigai is often described as what gets you out of bed in the morning. While this statement is certainly true, I believe ikigai is what excites you to want to wake up early the *following* morning. When we have something to look forward to—a first date, a movie we desperately want to see, the start of a holiday adventure—it transforms the simple act of getting out of bed into something thrilling. It has you jumping out of bed like you did when you were a child on Christmas morning. What's giving your life zest right now?

DAY 35 • IKIGAI MOTIVATES YOU

Ikigai is the fuel that keeps you going along life's bumpy path. It's that inner motivation you feel pushing you to honor your values, achieve your goals, pursue your purpose, and persevere when things get tough. It is what will carry you through hardship and adversity. When there is an injustice you refuse to let pass in silence or a wrong you wish to right, ikigai will motivate you to take the first step. What is ikigai—that inner voice—encouraging you to change about yourself or the world around you? What would be the first step to take?

DAY 36 • IKIGAI CONNECTS YOU

Ikigai connects you to the people who matter to you. It gives you that warm, fuzzy feeling you share with others, making you feel connected. It's the desire to express intimacy: emotional, intellectual, and spiritual. It's that moment when you have the desire to share a small joy or good news with a family member or friend. That's ikigai encouraging you to communicate freely like you did when you were a child, joyfully from the heart. What's some good news you've been wanting to share? Who's the person you want to share it with? Call them today.

DAY 37 • IKIGAI PROTECTS YOU

Ikigai can be a place to escape to, both literally or metaphorically. It can be a physical spot that gives you comfort, like a cozy sofa or your favorite café full of familiar faces. Or it can be the memory of a person or special moment that shields you from the chaos and uncertainty of the modern world. Ikigai gives you a focus on the things that are meaningful, beautiful, and awe-inspiring in your life and the world around you. What's a memory or place you can escape to when anxiety or overwhelm takes hold?

DAY 38 • IKIGAI REMINDS YOU

Ikigai reminds you of what matters in life. It is easy to get lost in life when each day blurs into the next. Ikigai brings back into focus what and who matters to you—from small joys and meaningful experiences to the people you often find yourself thinking of and wanting to talk to. It also reminds you not to take life too seriously, and urges you to make the most of life's fleeting opportunities and appreciate them. What is your ikigai reminding you is important as you reflect on this?

DAY 39 • IKIGAI FREES YOU

Ikigai empowers you to be yourself and embrace a carefree spirit. When you live with ikigai, you allow yourself to be playful and spontaneous. You can be yourself, free to act the way you want, say what you want, and be the natural you without concern for other people's agendas, personal politics, or opinions. Ikigai gives you the opportunity to focus on what matters to you and express your uniqueness. What playful activity would give you a sense of freedom today?

DAY 40 • IKIGAI MAKES YOU *YOU*

Ikigai is what makes you who you are. It's the accumulation of your life experiences, your values, interactions with people who have influenced you, events that have shaped you, and the dreams and goals that guide your future. All of these elements converge to form who you are. If you want to understand yourself, look at your ikigai sources. What do they reveal about you? And if you feel you don't yet know yourself, explore life to uncover more ikigai: the things that truly matter to you.

DAY 41 • THE SUFFIX GAI

Ikigai is not the only word Japanese use when talking about the things they value in life. In addition to *ikigai*, there are also other words, *yarigai, hatarakigai, asobigai* , *manabigai,* and *oshiegai* —all things that hold "value" or "worth," as shown by the use of the suffix *-gai*. We could consider ikigai an umbrella term for all of these words—words we will explore in this chapter—which seamlessly integrate into our day-to-day living to bring us joy and meaning. What do you value in life?

DAY 42 • YARIGAI • やりがい

Yarigai means "something worth doing." Where ikigai is more psychological and philosophical, yarigai is more practical and immediate. If something is worth doing, the Japanese will use the expression *yarigai ga aru*. *Aru* means "is" or "exists," and *ga* acts as a subject marker. The phrase *yarigai ga aru* indicates that something holds value or is worth doing. Something worth doing makes life feel more purposeful. What's one activity that is worth doing for you today?

DAY 43 • ASOBIGAI • 遊びがい

Asobi is the noun form of the verb *asobu*, meaning "to play," "to have fun," or "to engage in recreational activities." As you know, the suffix *gai* conveys the idea of "worth," "value," or "reward." By combining these two elements, *asobigai* can be interpreted as "the value of play" or "rewarding play," suggesting that play is not just enjoyable but also meaningful and fulfilling. However, asobigai is a word almost never spoken or written by Japanese people. Perhaps this needs to change, as the word can help us identify hobbies and leisure activities that are life-affirming. What hobbies in your life encapsulate the essence of asobigai or play?

DAY 44 • HATARAKIGAI • 働きがい

The phrase *hatarakigai* is used to indicate "work that is worth doing." This often involves engaging in work that is both challenging and demanding—not always enjoyable, but ultimately satisfying. It is important to understand that hatarakigai is a balance of both intrinsic and extrinsic motivators. It is all too easy for us to do work that is merely a means to an end, rather than something we are intrinsically motivated to do because we find value in it. Have you ever felt deeply satisfied with a project or task? If you're feeling disconnected from work, what are some steps you can take to rekindle a sense of purpose?

DAY 45 • MANABIGAI • 学びがい

To have ikigai is to have a love of learning. And a love of learning involves *manabigai*—"meaningful learning." The feeling of excitement, growth, and inspiration you can gain from learning makes life feel worth living. This may be the very reason you have this book in your hands. What we learn shapes our lives and the people we become. We do what we learn. We become what we learn. All of this then raises the question: What do you want to learn?

DAY 46 • OSHIEGAI • 教えがい

The Japanese verb for "to teach" is *oshieru*; thus, "the value of teaching" is expressed as *oshiegai*. This term can refer both to the subject that is worth teaching and to the character of the person who you feel is worth investing your time in. Ikigai is often found in the act of teaching, as it allows us to invest and contribute to someone's growth. What life wisdom have you acquired that is worth sharing with others? Alternatively, is there someone you know who needs support with their education? Could you support them in some way?

DAY 47 • TSUKURIGAI • 作りがい

Tsukurigai is a compound of the verb *tsukuru*, meaning "to make," "to create," or "to craft." Tsukurigai is often associated with cooking—more specifically, cooking dishes that are worth the time and effort to make because of the joy and satisfaction they bring to others. Tsukurigai also conveys the sense of fulfillment that comes from making or creating something. It suggests that an activity engaging your creativity to produce something unique will be meaningful, satisfying, or rewarding. Tsukurigai asks the question: What is worth creating?

DAY 48 • YOMIGAI • 読みがい

I hope you find this book worth reading. If you do, then it holds *yomigai* for you. Something worth reading not only provides insight, perspective, wisdom, and enjoyment, but also connects you to the author. The four-character idiom *dokusho-shōyū* (読書尚友) conveys the idea of forming friendships with ancient sages through reading. *Dokusho* (読書), the act of reading, allows you to travel back in time and befriend great minds of the past, which is the essence of *shōyū* (尚友). What inspiring figure from the past would you like to befriend? If they wrote a book, read it. If they didn't, read their biography—or, if none exists, seek out the stories told about them (journals, letters, reflections, etc.).

DAY 49 • TAYORIGAI • 頼りがい

Do others such as family, coworkers, and friends depend on you? If they do, then you have *tayorigai*, the quality of being someone others can rely on. When others count on you and you feel needed, then you're very likely to feel a strong sense of ikigai. Knowing that you matter brings a sense of significance and meaning to your life. With tayorigai you know you have a place in this world. Who depends on you? In what ways does being needed give your life meaning?

G
A
I

DAY 50 • SHINIGAI • 死にがい

With life comes the acceptance of death. One day, our lives will end. The word *shinigai* means "reason to die"—a death worth dying for. Shingai is not about glorifying death; rather, it points to the idea that a meaningful death completes a meaningful life. Some people willingly risk their lives, and some have given their lives for what they love or believe in: to protect others, to stand up for justice, or to care for those in need. Think of people whose final acts were defined by courage, compassion, and a commitment to others. What would you say to them?

神谷美恵子

Mieko Kamiya

DAY 51 • THE MOTHER OF IKIGAI

Mieko Kamiya was one of the first academics to extensively study ikigai. Her seminal book, *Ikigai ni Tsuite* (*About Ikigai*), is still considered a standard reference by contemporary Japanese researchers, professors, and psychologists, despite being published over a half-century ago in 1966. In the introduction of her book, she asks readers two questions: What makes us feel that life is worth living each and every day? How do we find a new ikigai if we have lost our reason to live? Reflect or journal on these questions.

DAY 52 • THE SEVEN IKIGAI NEEDS

Kamiya identified seven essential ikigai needs that contribute to a meaningful life: life satisfaction, the feeling of fulfillment in daily existence; change and growth, the pursuit of personal development; a bright future, a sense of hope and optimism; resonance, the ability to connect deeply with others; freedom, the autonomy to make choices; self-actualization, expressing one's unique imagination; and meaning and value, role and contribution. These needs, now central to positive psychology, highlight how purpose and well-being are deeply intertwined. Kamiya's insights continue to shape modern discussions on life's meaning. Which of these seven ikigai needs resonate with you the most at this moment?

DAY 53 • LIFE SATISFACTION

Life satisfaction is the most fundamental need. It can be met when someone feels that their life is moving in a better direction or toward a better state. Extroverts can satisfy the need for a sense of life satisfaction by being proactive in life, engaging in many tasks, and maintaining many relationships. Introverts, on the other hand, often find deep life satisfaction in quiet, personal pursuits that reflect their inner world. They may choose to nurture close-knit relationships, often prioritizing meaningful connections with family. What brings you life satisfaction? What makes you feel your life is moving forward?

DAY 54 • CHANGE AND GROWTH

Boredom and apathy drain ikigai. When life starts to feel dull or meaningless, it's easy to slip into indifference and lose touch with what makes you feel alive. One way to avoid these anti-ikigai states is to welcome change and embrace new experiences—traveling, learning a craft, meeting new people. These pursuits tap into our natural drive to grow and push our limits, resulting in self-development. How do you wish to grow? What is your ikigai calling you to do?

DAY 55 • A BRIGHT FUTURE

Ikigai is closely tied to how you see your future, what you're excited about, and what you're working toward. Having things to look forward to—experiences, events, goals, or dreams—can give each day a sense of energy and direction. The brightness of your future depends on how you imagine it and what steps you're willing to take to bring it to life. Make a list of all the activities and adventures you'd love to experience in the next year. Then, choose one and take a symbolic step—like picking a date for a trip or signing up for a class—to show your commitment. Keep going through your list, turning ideas into plans.

DAY 56 • RESONANCE

Resonance is the need to feel that what you're doing connects with others and with the world around you. At its core, this is a need for social connection: the desire to build meaningful relationships and to feel accepted by others. One of the most powerful ways to meet this need is by dedicating yourself to someone important to you—by giving and receiving love. This is where the question shifts from "What is your ikigai?" to "Who is your ikigai?" Tell someone you love that they are your ikigai—that they make your life worth living. Don't wait to do this. Tell them today.

DAY 57 • FREEDOM

When we talk about the need for freedom in the context of ikigai, we're really talking about a sense of freedom. It's that feeling you get after summiting a mountain, when you stretch out your arms wide and breathe in the air. It's about connecting to a natural environment, a state of mind, or a sense of accomplishment that makes you feel truly free. It's a moment when you feel liberated from the demands and expectations of the artificial world. Reflect and write about moments in your life when you've felt free. Describe them in detail—where you were, what you were doing, who you were with, and what made those moments feel so liberating.

DAY 58 • SELF-ACTUALIZATION

Self-actualization involves the desire to bring something into the world that hasn't existed before with your unique imagination. More than just an achievement, it becomes a reflection of your uniqueness, a sign that your existence has meaning. To fulfill this need, you don't have to achieve something grand and world changing; you just have to create something new through your creativity. It can be something humble, like a poem, a piece of art, or a recipe you invent. What small offering do you want to bring into the world for others, like family and friends, to enjoy?

DAY 59 • MEANING AND VALUE

We all have a deep, often unspoken desire to feel that our lives have meaning and value. It's part of being human. Whether we realize it or not, we're constantly searching for meaning, sometimes asking ourselves, "Why am I doing this?" or, "Is this really me?" during activities we begin to find pointless. For ikigai to truly be felt, we need to engage in activities that affirm life—activities that make us feel alive, connected, and purposeful. Where in your life would you like to find more meaning? And when do you feel you're offering value to others, even in small ways?

DAY 60 • A SENSE OF PURPOSE

All of us, in one way or another, are guided by a sense of purpose—even if it's a little unclear or hard to put into words. It's that feeling that you were put on this planet for a reason. Searching for, finding, and then pursuing your unique purpose makes life worth living because you are taking responsibility for and making the most of your life. When you do that, you feel ikigai at the most profound level. Your life truly becomes worth living. Reflect deeply and write about what purpose or role you feel you were born to fulfill.

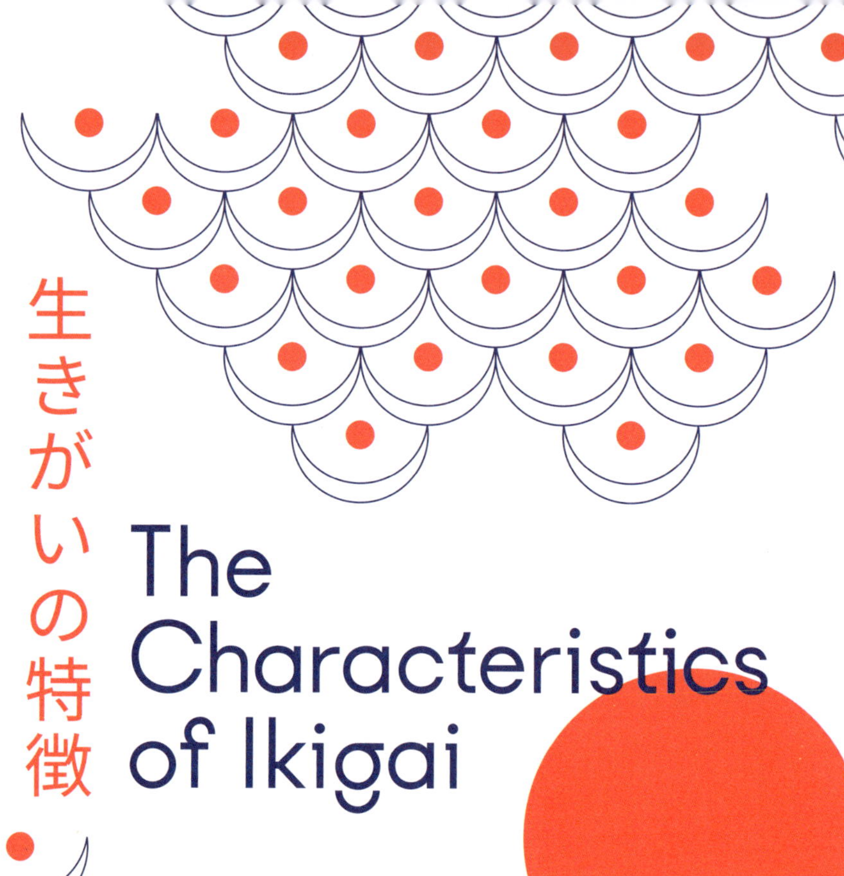

生きがいの特徴 The Characteristics of Ikigai

DAY 61 • A SOURCE OF IKIGAI

What makes an ikigai source an ikigai source? That is, what general characteristics do ikigai sources typically have? The answers to these questions vary from person to person. Some might define ikigai as something that allows them to feel the joy of being alive in a brief moment. Others might describe it as something that, upon reflection, always remains deeply embedded within them. However you wish to describe it, an ikigai source is something you assign meaning and value to. What gives you meaning? What do you value?

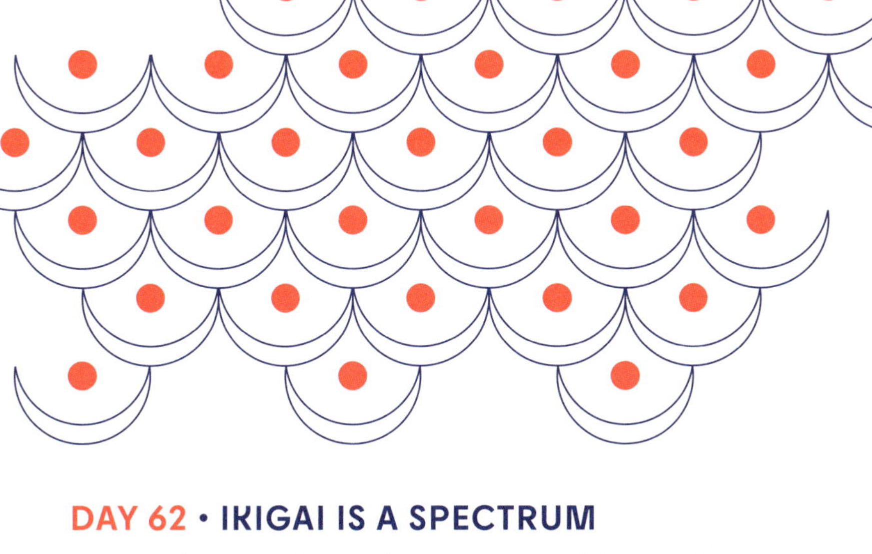

DAY 62 • IKIGAI IS A SPECTRUM

In Japan, ikigai is understood as a spectrum of the experiences, connections, and moments that make life feel meaningful. It might show up in the ways you care for others, the simple routines that bring comfort, the excitement of learning something new, or memories that warm your heart. Ikigai isn't a fixed destination; it's a personal mosaic of fulfillment shaped by what matters most to you. What small things can you add to your spectrum of ikigai?

DAY 63 • IKIGAI GIVES A PERSON IKIGAI-KAN

Ikigai-kan is the feeling you have when you have a zest for life. It is the feeling you have when you get uncontrollable giggles with an old friend. It's the feeling of warmth you experience when you hug someone you love. It's the feeling you have when you think your life is moving forward. It is the feeling you have when you overcome a struggle and discover your potential. Ikigai-kan is the emotional response to life experience that makes life feel worth living. What activities or relationships give you a zest for life?

DAY 64 • IKIGAI ACTIVITIES ARE DRIVEN BY SPONTANEITY

Ikigai is never driven by external pressure; it arises naturally from your inner desires. Ikigai often involves spontaneous activities which you undertake willingly. There is no hesitation when it comes to ikigai. Ikigai is something you simply feel like doing, often on the spur of the moment. What is that for you?

DAY 65 • IKIGAI IS ENTIRELY INDIVIDUAL

Ikigai cannot be borrowed or imitated from others. Your ikigai is a reflection of your true self, aligning with your values and what you hold dear in life. When it comes to ikigai, there is no need to think the grass is greener on the other side. Those who experience true ikigai do not compare theirs to someone else's. It would never cross their mind. Like the Japanese proverb, "Ten people, ten colors," your ikigai has its own color, which is uniquely yours.

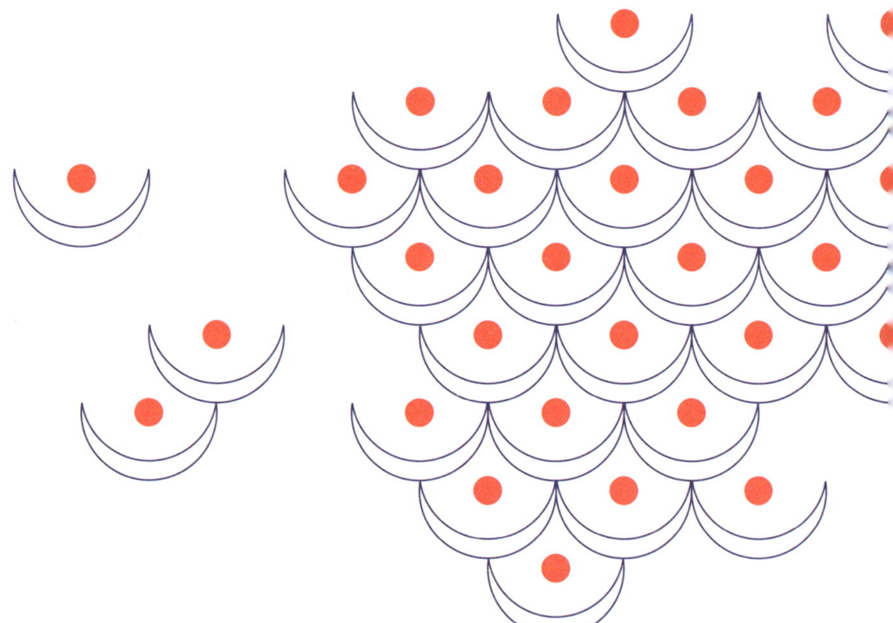

DAY 66 • IKIGAI DEVELOPS YOUR VALUE SYSTEM

If you have multiple sources of ikigai, you are likely to establish a hierarchy of priorities with the ikigai sources you value most. This makes decision-making easy and gives you a pecking order of what to do when life becomes a struggle. Often, this hierarchy goes unnoticed in daily life but becomes clearer when life throws you a curveball. This value system feeds back to your ikigai, creating a virtuous loop. As a result, life becomes more fulfilling as it becomes evident to you which decisions are right for your ikigai.

DAY 67 • IKIGAI FOSTERS A UNIQUE MENTAL WORLD

Along with a value system, ikigai creates a mental world, an ikigai mindset, where you gain clarity on what matters and what you want to focus your thoughts on. The clearer you are about what matters to you—your sources of ikigai—the more certainty you'll have in making meaning of your life. In short, ikigai provides the conditions for peace of mind because you're not at a loss when it comes to what gives your life meaning and purpose. This ikigai mindset fosters a positive and optimistic worldview.

DAY 68 • FIRST-PERSON IKIGAI

According to Japan's Health-Ikigai Creation Advisors, who help retired individuals transition from a work-centered life to a new social life of meaning and purpose, ikigai can be uncovered in three domains: first-, second-, and third-person perspective ikigai. First-person perspective ikigai refers to an individually focused form of ikigai. This type of ikigai often involves pursuing self-improvement and personal growth by enhancing one's skills and taking on challenging tasks. Examples include aspiring to create beautiful paintings, practicing poetry, immersing oneself in pottery, or finding joy in cooking. What makes up your first-person sources of ikigai?

DAY 69 • SECOND-PERSON IKIGAI

Second-person ikigai refers to ikigai sources experienced in personal relationships, especially with intimate others like family members or friends. This type of ikigai involves finding value and meaning through shared experiences. The relationship is a source of ikigai, as is the shared activity. Examples offered by Japan's Health-Ikigai Creation Advisors include traveling with a partner, enjoying quality time with friends through activities like walking, and fostering family togetherness by sharing household responsibilities. These activities can be understood as shared sources of ikigai. Who and what shared activities make up your second person sources of ikigai?

DAY 70 • THIRD-PERSON IKIGAI

Third-person ikigai is found and experienced by being of service to others. It involves altruistic thinking and actions, and finding meaning in contributing to our extended family, community, or society at large. Examples of third-person perspective ikigai include activities such as community involvement and volunteering, obtaining qualifications and teaching others, engaging in welfare work, and taking care of others' needs. This is a purpose-driven ikigai that essentially creates a new role and a new lease on life for individuals willing to step into it. What new roles could become your third-person sources of ikigai?

生きがいの価値観 Ikigai Values

DAY 71 • UNIVERSAL CONCEPT

Ikigai is a universal concept, yet the Japanese language seems to be the only language with a single word to articulate it. This aligns with Sir Francis Galton's lexical hypothesis, which proposes that essential personality traits within a culture become embedded in its language. The more significant the trait, the more likely it is to be expressed in a single word. Ikigai is driven by cultural values. This is why, in Japan, ikigai is often experienced in the small and humble, while in the West, it is chased as a singular life purpose. Let's explore the values that shape ikigai in Japan. But first, consider the values that shape your life. What are the values that determine your ikigai sources?

DAY 72 • AWARENESS

The simple act of being aware brings more ikigai into your life. With this awareness, you begin to see a world of ikigai around you, from small joys and nature's fleeting moments to new opportunities and dreams waiting to be pursued. You realize how much you have to live for. The secret to cultivating more ikigai lies in staying present and holding a lingering mind that focuses on what is life-affirming. What is one source of ikigai you often overlook but could begin to appreciate more?

DAY 73 • ACCEPTANCE

Happiness, growth, life satisfaction, freedom, and self-actualization all start with acceptance: of yourself, of others, and of the world you live in. This is articulated by the Japanese word *arugamama*, which literally translates to "as it is." Arugamama means the acceptance of the true nature of things. Once you accept the true nature of things you can focus on the one thing you can control: your own actions. We all know that, pleasant or unpleasant, emotions eventually pass, and if you can focus on your actions, you can move forward with your life. Where do you struggle with acceptance in your life? What action could you take to move past this?

DAY 74 • GRATITUDE

Gratitude is so deeply woven into Japanese culture that it has daily expressions to convey it. One such expression is *itadakimasu*, meaning "I humbly receive," said before a meal. While it expresses appreciation toward those who prepared the food and the meal itself, it also carries the deeper meaning of "receiving life"— from an animal, a fruit, a grain — that will now sustain your life. Saying itadakimasu is an expression of ikigai, a moment of recognition, felt as fulfillment and gratitude for being alive. What are you grateful for? Start writing a list and see how long it goes.

DAY 75 • HUMILITY

Do you like to talk things up? While we all have the desire to share our good news and achievements, it can be a cheap source of ikigai to be boastful of our successes and good luck. Remaining humble and considerate of the needs of others is a form of compassionate ikigai where your focus extends beyond yourself. Recognizing and expressing gratitude for those who have contributed to your achievements is an act of ikigai that allows you to honor both others and the good fortune in your own life. Who do you have to thank for your recent achievements and successes?

DAY 76 • RESILIENCE

Do you love a challenge? You'll uncover more ikigai in life if you do. Resilience unlocks the door to a deeper understanding of life and of yourself. Overcoming challenges helps you discover your potential and brings you closer to your actualized self.
This deepens your sense of meaning and purpose. Because ikigai is fundamentally experiential, it arises not only from joyful moments, but also from difficult ones. These struggles can give rise to ikigai-kan, the sense that life is not just worth living, but worth fighting for. What new challenges are you ready to embrace to grow your resilience?

DAY 77 • MA • 間

Ma is an essential concept in understanding Japanese culture and art. Ma refers to a space intentionally left open or a silence deliberately maintained, allowing the moment to be felt and appreciated rather than filled. From music and performing arts to architecture, interior design, and even everyday conversation, ma is the intentional gap or pause that allows a space or moment to hold meaning and beauty. It is the space where a calm sense of ikigai can arise, where less is felt as more. Where can you create more space and silence in your life to feel more connected and present?

DAY 78 • HARMONY

Harmony is perhaps Japan's most prized cultural value, with its kanji character 和 *wa* literally meaning "Japanese style." Rather than focusing on individualism and personal freedom, wa emphasizes harmony and peaceful relationships—with others, within society, and with nature. This reduces concerns about the ego and minimizes friction in relationships, where no one feels more important than another. The result is a feeling of ikigai born from a deep sense of connection and belonging. In what relationships or areas of your life are you seeking more harmony? What could be your first step toward creating it?

DAY 79 • RESPECT

Who do you respect? What do you respect? The answer is your ikigai. Your sources of ikigai are the people you love and admire, the experiences you value and cherish, and the things you hold dear. Ikigai is what you respect; that's why it should never be taken for granted. To uncover more ikigai in your life, we can take inspiration from Japan and choose to honor others, and the opportunities life offers, with greater respect. Who or what have you been neglecting that deserves more respect? What person or aspect of your life would you like to honor?

生きがいの源泉

Ikigai Sources

DAY 80 • JAPAN'S TOP IKIGAI SOURCES

A recent survey studying ikigai among Japanese people found that fulfillment is often rooted in everyday experiences rather than in major accomplishments. Participants reported that simple moments—like enjoying daily routines, connecting with loved ones, or pursuing personal interests—held the most meaning. These insights offer a glimpse into how small, consistent joys can collectively shape a life that feels worthwhile. What small daily experiences bring meaning to your routine?

DAY 81 • EATING DELICIOUS FOOD

The ikigai source that many Japanese people stated as their number one was food. And it's easy to see why—Japan boasts an abundance of culinary delights: sushi, ramen, tempura, yakitori, and so much more. Since food is something we naturally crave, it's no surprise that eating delicious meals evokes a deep sense of ikigai. Food offers sensory pleasure, satisfaction, and comfort. What food is at the top of your ikigai list? As you think about it, what are your taste buds longing to savor right now?

DAY 82 • TRAVEL

Japanese people are big domestic travelers and Japan offers many fascinating destinations, prefectural festivals, cultural activities, historical locations, and *meibutsu*—regional specialties such as local foods, unique products, or handmade crafts. Japan is certainly a destination that I recommend you visit at least once in your lifetime. Travel sets us free, taking us on a journey of new sights, sounds, and smells, and offering a whole new world of ikigai to discover and enjoy. What is your next ikigai travel destination?

DAY 83 • ONSEN • 温泉

Japan embraces its bathing culture wholeheartedly—elevating the long, hot soak to a cultural ritual through its local *sentō* (public bathhouses) and *onsen* (natural hot springs). In a society that deeply values personal privacy, it might seem paradoxical to undress and bathe alongside strangers. Yet, for many, this shared experience brings a profound sense of ikigai. It's their way of unwinding, recharging, and returning to themselves. How do you relax, refresh, and rejuvenate?

DAY 84 • MUSIC

Music can make you lose control, triggering various responses in your brain to release dopamine and other neurotransmitters that evoke pleasure and excitement. It literally and emotionally moves you. Music also brings people and cultures together, transcending the limits of language to offer more than words can say. What music moves you? What particular song makes you feel ikigai? Take a moment to listen to it today.

DAY 85 • GOING OUT WITH FAMILY

For Japanese families, spending time with each other running errands or on a day out ranked as their top relationship-based ikigai. Going out with family breaks routine and creates a more engaging context or environment for role fulfillment and discussion. It keeps family relationships fresh. Who from your family can you spend time with this week?

DAY 86 • KEEPING IN TOUCH WITH FAMILY

As social creatures we naturally desire connection, especially with family. Having a chat with or staying in touch with family is a familiar and easy ikigai check-in producing feelings of comfort, coziness, and reassurance that someone you love is safe and well. Who from your family would appreciate an ikigai check-in from you today?

DAY 87 • TV AND MOVIES

We're wired to love stories—and movies and TV shows make them come alive. A good series often sparks lively conversations among friends or coworkers. These passive forms of ikigai offer us a brief escape from the stresses of daily life, helping us unwind and reset. But some films go beyond simple entertainment—they move us deeply or prompt reflection on life's bigger questions. So go ahead, treat yourself to a movie night or dive into a series binge this weekend. You've earned it.

DAY 88 • GETTING A GOOD NIGHT'S SLEEP

A good night's sleep is indeed a source of ikigai in and of itself, with the added benefit of fueling your ikigai the next day. A poor night's sleep drains the energy needed to create and express ikigai in daily life. Make going to bed an ikigai practice: Dim the lights, play soothing music, and engage in a reflective ritual such as journaling, noting down moments of gratitude from the day you've just lived. Turn sleep into a source of ikigai.

DAY 89 • WORK AND CHILD-REARING

Unsurprisingly, work ranks among the top ten sources of ikigai for Japanese men, offering a strong sense of purpose and role fulfillment—especially in their identity as providers. For Japanese women, raising children was cited as their most significant ikigai-related role. Though both roles can be demanding and come with their share of frustration and stress, they serve as powerful sources of meaning, purpose, and emotional depth. We all have roles that stretch us and challenge us, but also leave us feeling deeply fulfilled. What's one role in your life that does that for you?

DAY 90 • WATCHING SPORTS AND SUPPORTING IDOLS

Concerts and sporting events offer us a collective ikigai experience, where we feel a sense of belonging as we witness the sublime and awe-inspiring in the company of thousands. These moments are more than just entertainment—they tap into something deeply emotional and energizing. Whether it's singing along to a beloved anthem or cheering for an underdog victory, we feel connected, alive, and uplifted. The shared passion creates a sense of unity, even among strangers. What musician or sports star inspires you? What is it about their artistry, determination, or charisma that resonates with you and sparks your ikigai?

The Ikigai-9 Scale

DAY 91 • THE IKIGAI-9

A tool we can use to understand ikigai's multifaceted nature is the ikigai-9 scale, a psychometric tool originally published in 2012 by three psychology researchers at Tokyo's Mejiro University: Tadanori Imai, Hisao Osada, and Yoshitsugu Nishimura. The ikigai-9 offers a means of measuring ikigai across three dimensions: optimistic and positive emotions toward life, active and positive attitudes toward one's future, and the acknowledgment of the meaning of one's existence. Essentially, these three dimensions ask you to consider the emotions you feel, the future you envision, and your sense of self in relation to living life. Each of these dimensions are measured by nine statements, which we'll explore over the next nine days.

DAY 92 • I'M INTERESTED IN MANY THINGS

Ikigai is found in the variety of interests you already hold close. In today's wired world, it's easy to get lazy and slip into a passive routine of doomscrolling. Staying curious and engaged in many pursuits keeps you on your toes, grateful for what you already have, and open to new ikigai opportunities. Look at your life today and list three to five interests, big or small, that bring excitement and satisfaction to your days.

DAY 93 • I WOULD LIKE TO LEARN SOMETHING NEW OR START SOMETHING

Learning something new or starting something often comes with excitement and intrinsic motivation, as the process of learning is rewarding in and of itself. It also sets you on a path of growth and self-actualization as you begin to understand the potential that lies within you. What's something you've always wanted to learn? It could be a recipe, a hands-on skill, or a language. The beauty is that you get to decide.

DAY 94 • I WOULD LIKE TO DEVELOP MYSELF

By developing yourself, you move closer to the person you want to be. This involves setting goals, seeking challenges, and embracing opportunities for learning and growth. This attitude fosters resilience as you continually push beyond your comfort zones, taking the next step in cultivating your potential. Developing yourself not only benefits you, but also benefits others and society at large through the unique contributions you make as you change and grow. How would you like to develop yourself to get closer to the person you want to be? What small goal can you make for yourself to accomplish this week?

DAY 95 • I FEEL THAT I'M CONTRIBUTING TO SOMEONE OR TO SOCIETY

Contributing to someone or to society can be your gift of ikigai to others. Whether you impact one person or thousands, what's important is that you feel your contribution matters. A person who feels that they are contributing understands that they are part of something bigger, no matter how small their contribution or role is. How do you want to contribute to others and society today?

THE IKIGAI-9 SCALE

DAY 96 • I BELIEVE THAT I HAVE SOME IMPACT ON SOMEONE

We want to believe and feel that what we do matters, that we bring about positive changes. However, it's not about size or numbers—influencing even one person in a life-changing way is meaningful. It is astounding how the most fleeting of thoughts and smallest of actions can set in motion events that dramatically impact the course of our lives. Recognize the impact you've had on others this week with some journaling. This is not about feeding your ego; it's about acknowledging what you've done for others with a sense of positivity.

DAY 97 • MY EXISTENCE IS NEEDED BY SOMETHING OR SOMEONE

Many Japanese frame ikigai as being or feeling needed. As social beings, we crave belonging and long for a place in groups or communities where we can be authentic and accepted. These connections deepen our sense of self-worth and empower us to take on meaningful roles, giving us identity, purpose, and hope for the future. We may also experience a profound sense of purpose when we feel needed by a higher power, believing that we have been chosen for a special mission. Moving forward, how and by whom do you want to be needed?

DAY 98 • MY LIFE IS MENTALLY RICH AND FULFILLED

If ikigai had a goal, it would be that you live a mentally rich and fulfilling life. But what does this entail? A mentally rich life is one characterized by intellectual, emotional, experiential, and spiritual depth. It goes beyond surface-level pleasures or routines, encompassing meaningful relationships, engaging activities, and the expression of one's personal value system. A fulfilled life is lived with intention and balance, providing both joy and a sense of progress in various domains. This week, plan to include enriching and fulfilling activities. What's sparking your interest at the moment?

DAY 99 • I OFTEN FEEL THAT I'M HAPPY

Happiness is fundamental to our well-being, and feeling it often would constitute a life of ikigai. Yet, because happiness is inherently fleeting, the relentless pursuit of it is unwise. We all know it comes and goes, but its presence makes life worth living. To cultivate happiness more frequently, we must appreciate what we already have—the sources that generate our happiness. For this, we can notice the conditions under which we are happy. Journal about the conditions that make you happy: the people you spend time with, the activities you engage in, the environments or settings you are in, and the associated feelings you experience.

DAY 100 • YUTORI—I HAVE ROOM IN MY MIND

I think of yutori as "the space to have peace of mind." It is a state where you feel mental clarity and freedom from overwhelming thoughts or worries. With yutori, you gain the space to reflect on life and consider others. In short, yutori is a sense of contentment—a state where you realize you need nothing more. The secret to creating yutori is to do less. In today's fast-paced world, where we are often preoccupied with our screens or distracted by constant demands, yutori is a state few of us experience daily. Many of us wait for weekends or holidays rather than cultivating it in our everyday lives. What can you unburden yourself from to give yourself more time to be free and present? What can you take off your to-do list?

DAY 101 • WHAT'S YOUR LEVEL OF IKIGAI?

For each of the statements on **Days 92 to 100** respond with one of the options: "⑤ Very applicable," "④ Quite applicable," "③ Somewhat applicable," "② Not very applicable," or "① Hardly applicable." Then add up your total score. This score will determine how close you are to the ideal ikigai tally of 45, giving you a sense of the level of ikigai currently present in your life. You can also look at which statements are lower than the possible 5/5 and identify which aspects of your life to focus on in order to increase ikigai-kan. What ikigai measure needs more of your attention and care?

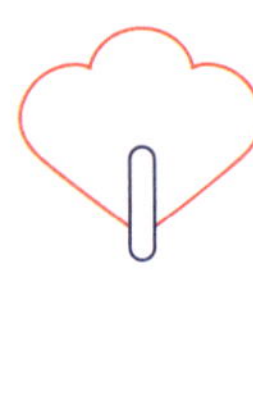

生きがいが見つかる場所

Where Ikigai Is Found

DAY 102 • IKIGAI IS FOUND IN THE SMALL

Ikigai is found in the everyday moments that make you pause and smile or laugh. It is found in the small familiar rituals that bring you comfort, like petting your cat when you return home. Perhaps this is ikigai's best kept secret and the most valuable lesson we can take away from the concept: you can find and feel plenty of ikigai in the small joys and simple pleasures of life. The secret is to be present to notice them. What small joys of ikigai are you blessed with?

DAY 103 • IKIGAI IS FOUND IN STILLNESS

Ikigai is found in stillness, when you stop to be fully present to an experience, environment, or situation. Stillness puts you in the now so you can immerse yourself in the moment. Like watching a beautiful sunset in silence or being mesmerized by a bird eating nectar from a flower, ikigai opens your eyes to the wonders of the world. Being in nature teaches us to be still to witness something beautiful; to not move and spook the miracles unfolding before our eyes.

DAY 104 • IKIGAI IS FOUND IN BANTER

Ikigai is found in the playful back-and-forth you have with someone you love, trust, and respect. It's when teasing is an expression of love that's immediately understood, received, and often reciprocated. This is a daily ikigai I share with my son. Banter colors our conversations, turning the mundane into the joyful, often generating laughter and the feeling of intimacy. Banter is an on-the-spot ikigai you can share with a true friend or loved one, proving that ikigai can be spontaneous. Who is your banter buddy?

DAY 105 • IKIGAI IS FOUND IN HUMOR

Do you notice that when we laugh, we laugh with our whole body? Without conscious control, our voice rhythmically explodes, our chest heaves in and out, our body shakes, and our face contorts. Humor triggers a full body experience, where we live so completely in the moment we have no control. Intense laughter can make our tummy ache and bring tears to our eyes, but we love the experience. This is ikigai tickling your heart, making life feel glorious for a brief but timeless moment. Who makes you laugh? Give them a call and have a chuckle.

DAY 106 • IKIGAI IS FOUND IN ANTICIPATION

What do you have to look forward to? Ikigai is felt as anticipatory pleasure, as the excitement for something you can't wait to experience or witness, similar to a child on Christmas Eve who can't wait for Santa. When the day or event draws near, you feel giddy, almost nervous, making it hard to sleep. Sometimes, the feeling is so intoxicating it's even more enjoyable than the event itself. The lesson here? Always have something to look forward to. Plan something exciting for the future, perhaps start by planning something for this weekend.

DAY 107 • IKIGAI IS FOUND IN NOSTALGIA

Ikigai can be an emotional bridge to your past, with fond memories generating intense feelings of nostalgia and longing. Looking back on life can revive a sense of ikigai. Nostalgia is so powerful it's used in reminiscence therapy, which involves conversations about past events, with personal items such as photos, keepsakes, or music used to evoke memories and positive emotions. You literally have a memory bank to reminisce on. Engage in a little personal reminiscence therapy today. Call an old friend and talk about the good old days or journal about some of your memories and see what brings a smile to your face or a tear to your eye.

DAY 108 • IKIGAI IS FOUND IN ART

Art, both the creation and appreciation of it, is an uplifting source of ikigai for many. The captured imagination and flow of the artist, whether in paintings, sculptures, architecture, or music, stirs our own imagination and holds our attention. This may be why artworks such as Michelangelo's *David*, da Vinci's *Mona Lisa,* and the prehistoric cave paintings in Chauvet are considered among humanity's greatest achievements. What artwork inspires awe within you? Is there an artist in you desiring to express itself?

DAY 109 • IKIGAI IS FOUND IN SPACE

Japanese culture values negative space. As I mentioned on **Day 77**, they have a word for it: ma. In Japan, ma is everywhere: in the openness of architecture, the white space of calligraphy, the performance of Noh and Kabuki theater, the brief pause of a bow of a formal greeting, and the comfortable silences of conversation—something many non-Japanese struggle with. Ma places you in the present. Ma honors the moment. Ma is the ikigai we feel but don't see. Where do you need to create more ma?

DAY 110 • IKIGAI IS FOUND IN OTHERS

Ikigai is found in others—in those wonderful moments we share with family, friends, familiar faces, and even strangers. Ikigai is interdependent. We need others—they give us relationships, roles to play, purpose to feel, and a life to live. Likewise, others need us for the same reasons. Who are the others you want to share ikigai with?

DAY 111 • IKIGAI IS FOUND IN YOUR WORDS

The language you've used in the past has shaped the life you live today. The words you speak now will determine the experiences of your days ahead. Optimism and positive language will bring more ikigai into your life. What's the ikigai of tomorrow that you want to experience? You need to speak it today. Ikigai language is life-affirming, with words full of positivity, optimism, and gratitude. It tells you when to say *thank you*, *I'm sorry*, and *I love you*—words from your heart. What words from the heart will you use this week? See how many times you can say thank you tomorrow.

DAY 112 • IKIGAI IS FOUND IN THE MISFORTUNE OF OTHERS

If we are honest with ourselves, the misfortunes of the people we don't like or don't get along with can put a spark in our step. Gloating about the misfortunes of others can make us feel ikigai—*your* misfortune makes *my* life feel better. The German language even has a word for this: *schadenfreude,*with *schaden* meaning "damage" and *freude* meaning "joy." And while we may think justice has been served to those we don't like, remember misfortune will visit you one day, too. What would it take for you to be understanding of and compassionate toward those you don't get along with?

DAY 113 • IKIGAI IS FOUND IN REVENGE

Ikigai is felt in the desire for revenge. If you have ever been taken advantage of or treated unfairly, feelings of hate and the desire for vengeance naturally come to the surface. Revenge is an instinctive impulse that's hard to control when others have humiliated or betrayed you. Enacting your revenge may feel justified and even satisfying when achieved, but this is an ikigai I encourage you not to express. Instead, practice forgiveness, compassion, and let the desire for revenge go. Who in your life would you like to bring yourself to forgive?

DAY 114 • IKIGAI IS FOUND IN COMMUNITY

Community gives us a place to belong and a chance to step into meaningful roles. When you contribute to others in a way that uses your unique talents and skills, you satisfy several ikigai needs, including the need for purpose and the need for belonging. Community also offers you the opportunity to grow and self-actualize into the person you feel you're meant to be. To become all we can be, we need community. What roles do you currently inhabit in your communities? What ikigai needs do these roles satisfy, and how do they shape who you are becoming?

DAY 115 • IKIGAI IS FOUND IN NATURE

The dance of a pollinating butterfly, the smell of cedar trees, the roar of a waterfall—nature offers an abundance of ikigai sources to remind us of the beauty and awe of Mother Nature. When we spend time in nature, we feel refreshed, rejuvenated, and healed from the overstimulation of the modern world. Nature is the Earth's wise mentor, reminding us that simply being still and observing the interplay of life around us affirms our own life and offers a kind of wisdom that can't be put into words. Plan a trip where you'll spend a day in nature. Document the experience with photos and some journaling.

DAY 116 • IKIGAI IS FOUND IN THE UNIVERSE

The universe—what little we know of it—has been a source of study and debate for thousands of years. Looking up at the night's sky is the closest we get to touching the universe, and the act often triggers existential questions: Why are we here? What is the meaning of life? Paradoxically, stargazing makes for a contemplative source of ikigai, one that makes us feel comfortable and connected despite knowing how small and insignificant we are in the vastness of the cosmos. Go stargazing with your family or friends and discuss the mysteries of the universe.

DAY 117 • IKIGAI IS FOUND IN LOVE

Ikigai is the feeling of being loved. We feel it when we are unconditionally loved by the people in our lives such as family and friends—when we are listened to, encouraged, praised, and hugged. Being treated this way makes us feel heard, valued, and safe. The love we received in the past and the love we feel now are ours to pass on. It's a gift of ikigai we can offer others, so they too can feel loved. Who will you show love to today? Who will make you feel valued?

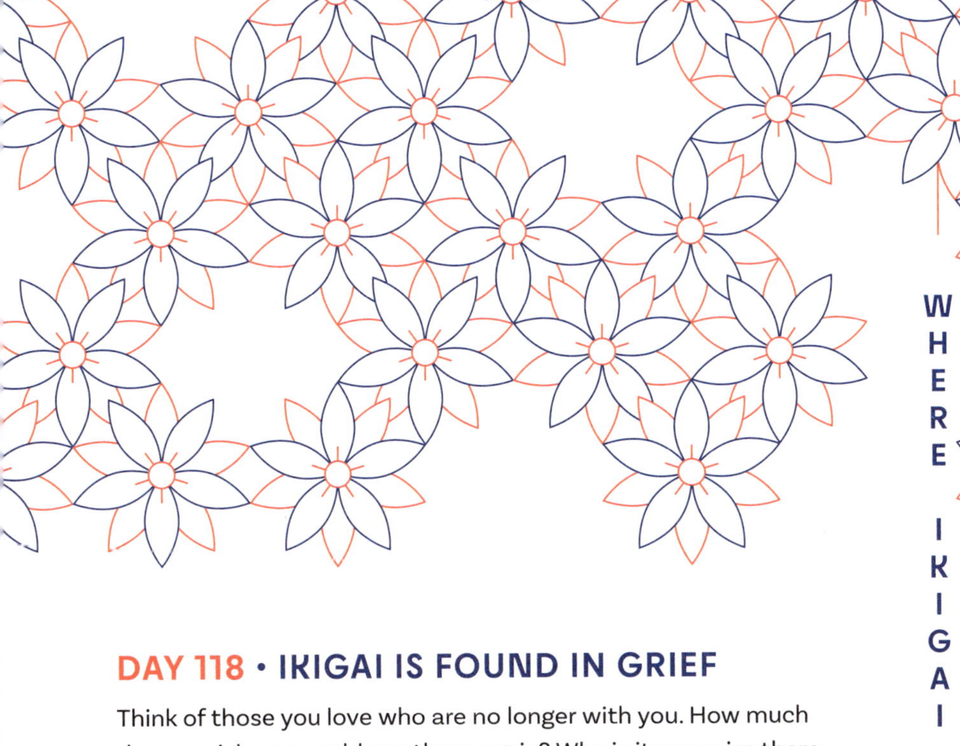

DAY 118 • IKIGAI IS FOUND IN GRIEF

Think of those you love who are no longer with you. How much do you wish you could see them again? Why is it you miss them so much? They were your ikigai. Tragically, sometimes it's only through losing others that we come to understand how much they mean to us. Grief is love yearning to be answered—yet you know it will never be, because it can't be received by the one you have lost. Grief mourns a lost source of ikigai. Who is someone you've lost you wish you could see again? Spend the day with them in your thoughts and memories.

DAY 119 • IKIGAI IS FOUND WITHIN YOU

You can find many ikigai sources in the world around you, but the most profound and meaningful sources are uncovered within you—in your personality, your creativity, and the qualities that make you who you are. Think of yourself as a source of ikigai. You matter because you create ikigai-kan for others, whether you know it or not. What are the qualities in you that others gravitate toward?

DAY 120 • IKIGAI IS FOUND IN DIVERSITY

Ikigai results from experiencing life and discovering what resonates with you. As you now know, it can take many forms—finding purpose through work, engaging in lifelong learning, playing sports, traveling, pursuing crafts, or simply spending time with people you care about. The more diverse your experiences and the more people you connect with, the more opportunities you have to discover new ikigai sources. Over the next month, challenge yourself to try new activities and connect with different people. Notice what excites you, inspires you, or leaves you feeling fulfilled.

DAY 121 • IKIGAI IS FOUND IN OVERCOMING HARDSHIP

It's important to understand that ikigai is not solely derived from positive experiences. Hardship also reveals what's important to you. In short, hardship uncovers your most authentic ikigai sources—the ones you'll endure adversity to protect and maintain. These are also the ikigai sources that help you develop a stronger sense of self. Hardship not only reveals your ikigai, but also your true self. Reflect and write about the hardships you have overcome that have brought you to where you are today. What did they teach you about yourself?

余暇 Leisure

DAY 122 • VALUED EXPERIENCES

The relationship between leisure and ikigai has been studied extensively by leisure expert Dr. Shintaro Kono of the University of Alberta. One key concept that his work has explored is *keiken* or valued experience—specifically, the different types of leisure experiences that we value and that, therefore, lead to life satisfaction, resulting in the state of ikigai-kan. Kono has identified four main keiken, or valued experiences, that make life worth living: *tanoshimi, ganbari, shigeki, and iyashi.*

DAY 123 • TANOSHIMI • 楽しみ

Tanoshimi means "enjoyment." It refers to valued experiences that are intrinsically attractive, such as connecting with nature, playing sports, socializing with friends, or enjoying sensory experiences like listening to music or eating. These activities provide you with the opportunity to become absorbed in the present moment and, you guessed it, feel ikigai. Where do you feel more enjoyment in your life?

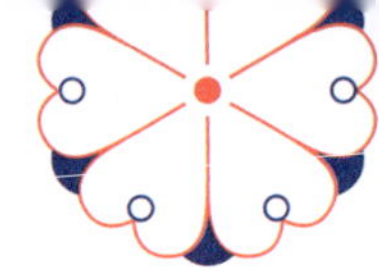

DAY 124 • GAMBARI • 頑張り

Gambari translates to "effort." As you would expect, effortful experiences are characterized by their challenging nature and can give you a sense of purpose as you strive to better yourself. Kono discovered that while effortful experiences often result in negative immediate outcomes such as setbacks, frustration, and stress, persevering through them leads to two positive long-term outcomes: self-enhancement and a sense of accomplishment. In other words, overcoming barriers is satisfying and fulfilling, leading to a truly unique feeling of ikigai-kan. What challenging leisure activities are worth making an effort in your life?

DAY 125 • SHIGEKI • 刺激

Shigeki, or "stimulation," is characterized by experiencing new activities, places, people, and ideas. These keep your daily life fresh and exciting and can radically transform your perspectives and even value system. Stimulation opens your eyes to opportunities, sparking curiosity and the desire to try something new. Shigeki is the spark that reveals a potential new ikigai source. Allowing your imagination to run wild, what new stimulating experiences would you like to try?

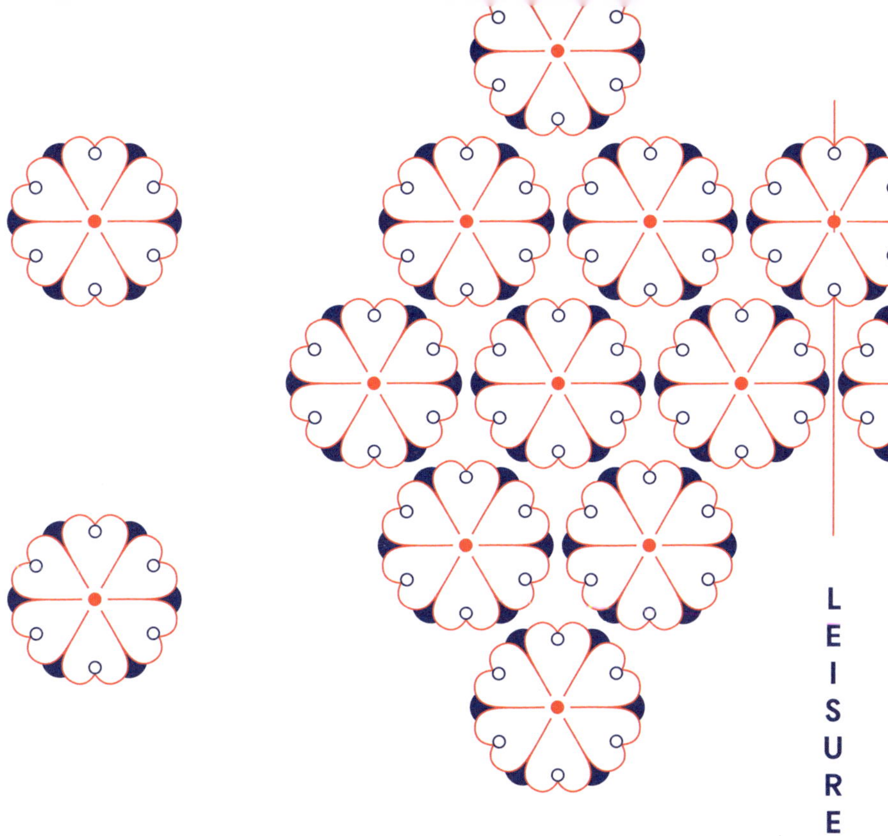

LEISURE

DAY 126 • IYASHI • 癒し

Iyashi means "comfort" and involves ordinary activities that take place in familiar places among friends and regular companions. These activities could include chatting over coffee or having picnics. When you are involved in comforting activities with people you know, you are free to be yourself, as you know you won't be judged or criticized. You are likely to spend a considerable amount of time engaged in these comforting activities, as they help you stay in tune with who you think you really are, reinforcing your sense of self. What shared activity brings you comfort? Can you make more time for it?

成長 Growth

DAY 127 • AWARENESS OF GROWTH

Change and growth give birth to ikigai. The moment we first became aware of our own growth most likely came with a strong sense of ikigai. Can you remember the first time you rode a bike without training wheels? For me, it came with an initial sense of disbelief, then an incredible sense of freedom. I could ride a bike and was no longer afraid of falling off it. Do you remember a time you experienced growth? What did it mean to you? Can you recall how you felt?

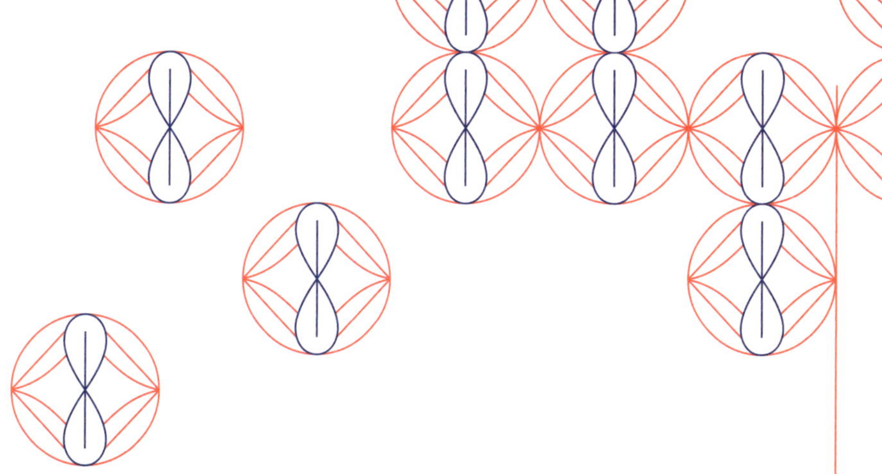

DAY 128 • MAKE A CHANGE

When you find yourself bored with life, treat the boredom with a change. Ikigai is the antidote to boredom. You can start small. Change what you drink in the morning, the route you take on your daily walk, or the music you listen to. As humans, we have a desire for new experiences. Boredom can indicate poor mental health, a state in which we feel that life has become stale. As a result, change becomes desirable. We want to avoid stagnation and boredom, and instead grow, which can only be achieved when we embrace change.

DAY 129 • HATSU • 初

Hatsu means "first" or "new" and expresses the idea of one's initial experience of life's many curiosities. Our first experiences in life are often the most impactful and meaningful. Our firsts make us grow, spark our curiosity, and sharpen our appetite for life. They can also be events or moments we wish we could forget, as they remind us of how cruel and unjust life can feel. It can be our first love, our first kiss, our first job, or our first loss. These firsts along our life journey shape the person we become, teach us lessons, and offer us the opportunity to grow. What firsts can you invite into your life today?

DAY 130 • KAIZEN • 改善

Kaizen means "change for better." According to the father of continuous improvement, Masaaki Imai, it is a concept that can be applied not only to business or one's working life, but also to one's personal life, home life, and social life. So, make better life choices. This can be anything from what you eat and drink to the type of media you consume. What changes can you make for the better?

DAY 131 • DON'T STOP; KEEP GOING

Growth not only comes from change but also from continuance. The Japanese proverb *keizoku wa chikara nari* (継続は力なり) translates to "continuation is power," meaning that growth and success can only come from the perseverance of continuation. It's easy to start a project or new hobby, but sustaining it with small efforts over time takes focus and determination. As this Japanese proverb reveals, "Raindrops will eventually carve through stone." It is the small, repeated efforts that lead to significant change and, more importantly, personal growth. Don't stop. Keep going.

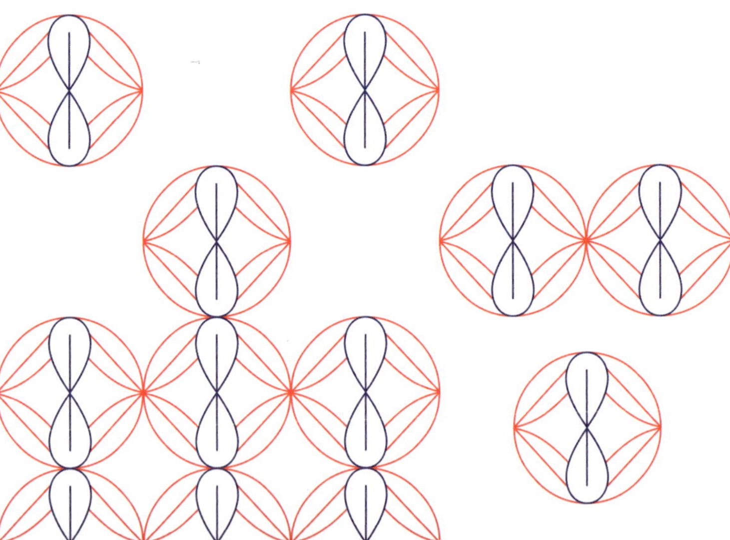

未来性

A Bright Future

DAY 132 • ALWAYS HAVE SOMETHING TO LOOK FORWARD TO

Make it a habit to find joy in what's ahead by scanning your calendar each week. Identify events, activities, or interactions that excite you, and highlight them as moments to inspire tanoshimi—the anticipation of happiness. If your schedule feels lacking, proactively plan something uplifting, like a chat with a friend or time for a personal passion. Make the simple act of recognizing what you have to look forward to a weekly practice. At the week's end, reflect on what feelings and life lessons these experiences and interactions gave you. You could make this a regular journaling practice.

DAY 133 • LIFE MOMENTUM

Do you feel that your life is moving forward? If you do, that is a feeling of ikigai. More specifically, it is the feeling Dr. Shintaro Kono calls life momentum. It is the connection of your current state—who you are, what you are doing, and what you value—to your future goals. Set and write out a new long-term goal—something that will take six months to a year to achieve. Give this goal deep thought. To feel a strong sense of ikigai in your life, set and pursue a goal that encourages you to express your values and creativity and challenges your abilities. The goal should be meaningful and require effort and commitment to create the state of life momentum.

DAY 134 • YOUR MIRROR

The proverb *mukashi wa ima no kagami* (昔は今の鏡) literally translates to "the past is a mirror for your now." The proverb reminds us that our past actions determine or reflect our present life and conditions, helping us understand and learn from our decisions. Perhaps more importantly, it tells us that whatever decisions or actions we take today will determine our future. As ikigai is something you can cultivate, what do you want to be looking at in your life's mirror five or ten years from now?

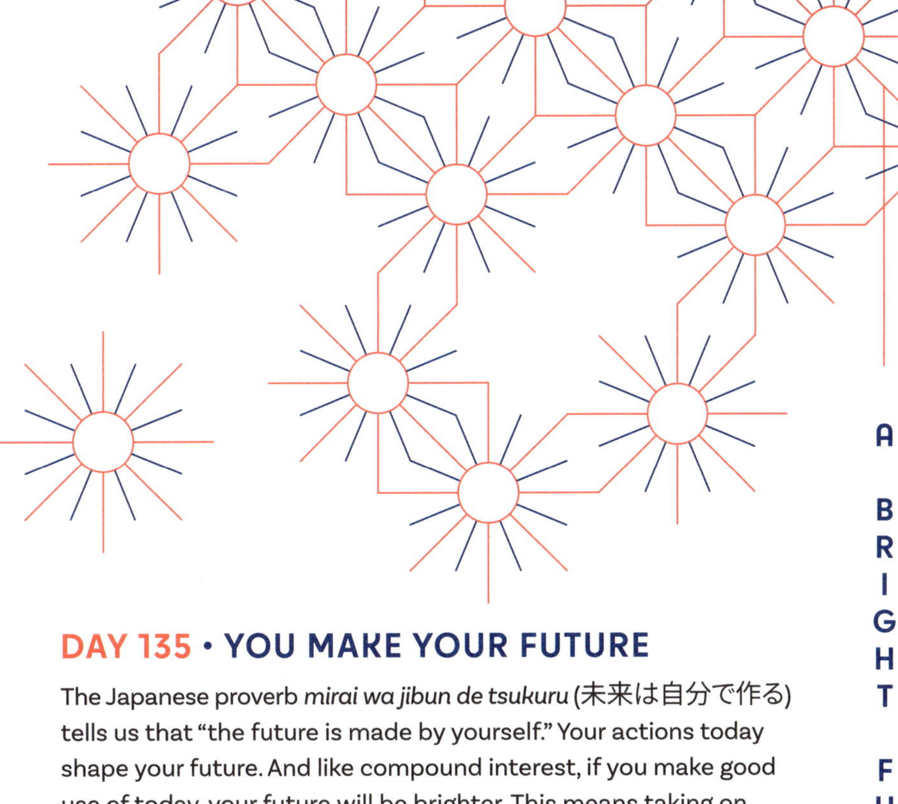

DAY 135 • YOU MAKE YOUR FUTURE

The Japanese proverb *mirai wa jibun de tsukuru* (未来は自分で作る) tells us that "the future is made by yourself." Your actions today shape your future. And like compound interest, if you make good use of today, your future will be brighter. This means taking on challenges, taking risks, and saying yes to opportunities when they arise. What is one thing you will say yes to this week?

DAY 136 • YOUR FUTURE SELF

Your future doesn't just get better when you make the most of today. You do, too. Are you the same person you were ten years ago? Most definitely not. You can kaizen yourself and make changes to become closer to the ideal version of the self you want to be. This takes reflection and foresight, a deep understanding of your values, and a vision of the person you want to become. You will live your future in the present when it comes. So your future is now. What do you want to do with it? In your journal, write about your future self—what you are doing, how you engage with others, how life feels, and so on.

反響 Resonance

DAY 137 • WHO MATTERS MOST?

What matters most to you—or, to rephrase the question slightly, who matters most to you? While our work, hobbies, goals, and dreams can be life-affirming sources of ikigai, it may be the people in your life—family, friends, colleagues, mentors—who are your strongest source of ikigai. These relationships may cause you to experience ikigai-kan most intensely. Write a letter of gratitude to the person that matters most to you, letting them know of the impact they have had on your life. You can choose to share it with them or keep it for yourself.

DAY 138 • INTIMACY

Relationships and connections with others can make you feel that life is worth living by generating feelings of intimacy—not only physical intimacy (though that is possible), but also emotional, intellectual, experiential, creative, and spiritual intimacy. Intimacy can lead to intense feelings of ikigai-kan because it makes you feel alive, causes you to lose yourself in a moment of connection, and provides you with life satisfaction, a sense of purpose, and a desire to keep making the most of life. What's an intimate moment, such as a hug or a playful conversation, you can share with someone today?

DAY 139 • ROLES

Roles are the parts we play as members of various social groups that resonate with society. Our roles give us the opportunity to express our values, feel a sense of purpose, and improve ourselves. Everyone is part of multiple social groups, and in each of those contexts, we may have a distinct, unique role. It is vital to identify and enact these roles because they keep us connected to other people and underpin our sense of worth and sense of self. Make a list of all of the roles you play in your day-to-day life. Which ones hold the most significance for you?

RESONANCE

DAY 140 • ROLEFULNESS

Rolefulness, a word coined by Professor Daiki Kato and Dr. Mikie Suzuki, is the ongoing sense of role satisfaction in daily life. It has two aspects: social rolefulness, based on social experiences and relationships with others, and internal rolefulness, a more internalized feeling that becomes the basis of cognition for individuality or confidence. There are three fundamental behaviors to help you cultivate rolefulness: exchanging greetings, having conversations, and expressing gratitude. Take a moment to engage in rolefulness by greeting someone warmly, starting a meaningful conversation, and expressing genuine gratitude. Reflect on how these simple acts enhance both your social connections and inner confidence.

DAY 141 • LOVE

Love, in all its forms, makes life worth living. We yearn for it when we don't have it. We often want to be loved by others so that we feel we matter. Yet, for us and others to feel it, we must love. We must care for others, give our time and attention, be patient, and listen, especially in those times when we feel we don't have the energy to do so. What is a loving thing you can do for someone else today?

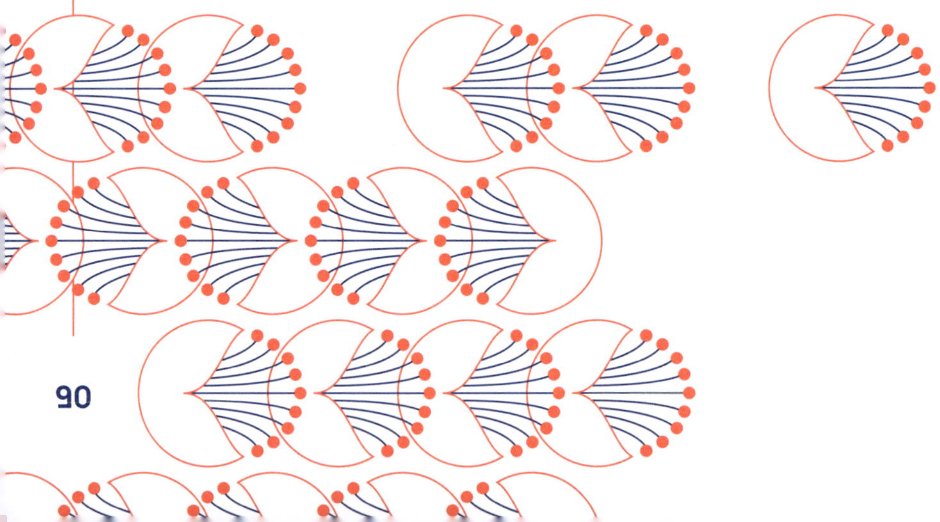

自由 Freedom

DAY 142 • THE FREEDOM OF CHOICE

When it comes to ikigai, you have freedom of choice. You're not bound by what others think should bring your life meaning. Ikigai isn't a rigid formula like a Venn diagram that you have to follow. It's personal, subjective, and entirely defined by you. You have the freedom to explore what gives your life meaning and the agency to decide what ikigai looks like for you. So be a little selfish with your ikigai. Make time for it. Treat yourself to an ikigai activity this week. Pamper yourself if you wish.

DAY 143 • THE PARADOX OF CHOICE

We now live in a world of excess with so many options that even simple decisions, like what clothes to buy or what show to watch, can lead to stress and fatigue. The freedom of choice has become a paradox of choice, where having too many options leads to anxiety rather than a sense of freedom. A Zen phrase, "Without desire, there is freedom," reflects the idea that by eliminating excessive desires, one can achieve true inner freedom. What desires or choices would you like to let go of? Write a list.

DAY 144 • KNOWING YOU HAVE ENOUGH

In Japanese culture, it is often believed that real freedom is experienced when you know you have enough. Our human desires are bottomless; the more we seek, the more unfulfilled we become, and thus, suffering arises. The proverb *taru o shiru* (足るを知る), "to know what is enough," emphasizes that true wealth and happiness come from recognizing and being satisfied with what one already possesses. In the context of freedom, it suggests that real freedom can be found in contentment and in not being overwhelmed by endless choices. Write out a list of things you are grateful for. How many things you add is up to you.

DAY 145 • DANSHARI • 断捨離

Danshari is a philosophy that aims to achieve a light and comfortable life by cutting off unnecessary items and eliminating attachment to material possessions. You might think of this as decluttering, but it is more of a mindset that seeks to attain a light and comfortable life by not only discarding possessions but also eliminating attachment. What is one thing that you could let go of today to create more mental freedom?

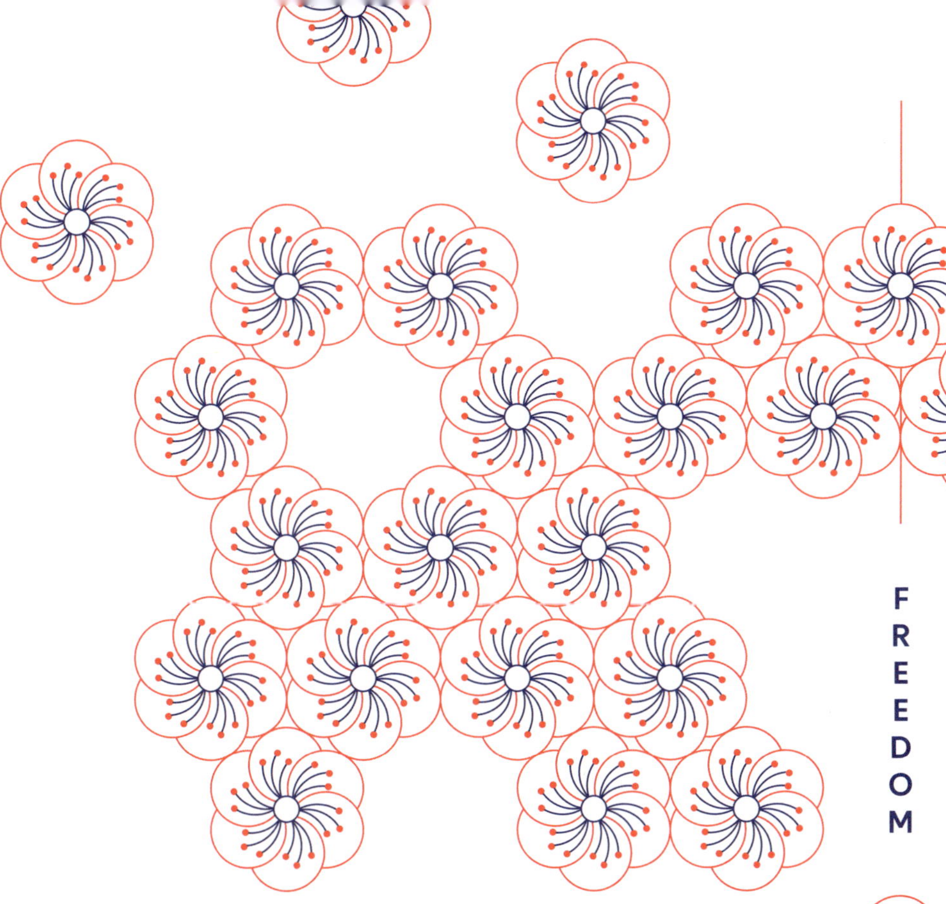

FREEDOM

DAY 146 • LET OTHERS BE FREE

Some parents, thinking they know what's best, end up destroying their children's freedom by trying to manipulate and mold them into the children they want them to be. This can have devastating long-term consequences for a child. We should never do this to others. Your freedom should never come at the expense of someone else's. It should never be an expectation for someone else to change. Let others be free to live authentically. How can you create space for the people in your life, be they your children or others, to express themselves freely, without expectations?

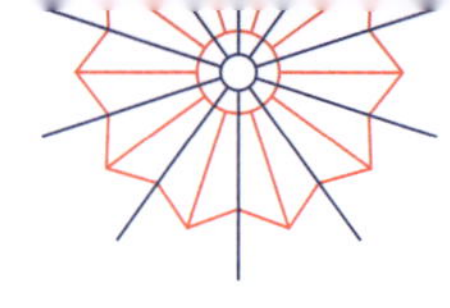

自己実現 Self-Actualization

DAY 147 • LIVING YOUR VALUES

You feel ikigai when you express your values. When you compromise or live in conflict with your values, then it's unlikely that you will feel ikigai in your day-to-day living. In relationships and roles, through one's work, and in creative pursuits, we feel ikigai because we are expressing our values. To self-actualize is to uphold one's values in the face of overwhelming pressure. What values matter most to you? How do you uphold these values?

DAY 148 • YOUR BEST SELF

In the West, there is a tendency to frame self-actualization, the process of becoming the most authentic and fulfilled version of yourself, as the pursuit of one's "best self." This typically involves a deficit model perspective, suggesting that a person's current way of being or doing is "wrong" or "lacking," but if these issues can just be addressed, self-actualization can be achieved—along with corresponding payoffs, such as financial gain, fame, and greater physical appeal. Ikigai isn't calling you to become your "best self." Instead, ikigai encourages you to do your best in the moment at hand.

DAY 149 • INTERDEPENDENCE, NOT INDEPENDENCE

In the West, we pride ourselves on being independent and tend to see dependence on others as a weakness. In the Japanese culture, it is understood that one's identity is derived from being a part of a whole, and that we belong to various groups—family, community, and society. These interpersonal relationships allow us to feel that we have a proper place in society. In Japan, self-authenticity and self-actualization go beyond the individual; it is believed we become ourselves with the help of others. Spend more time with the people who help you grow and actualize.

DAY 150 • ACCEPT YOURSELF

To become your true self, you must first accept yourself by releasing the ego—the part of you concerned with self-esteem or self-importance. The self that is constantly preoccupied with itself is not what matters. What matters is the self within you that can act freely, connect with others, and be playful. Write about yourself as if you were writing about your best friend. Focus on the qualities you admire and explore how your flaws make you unique rather than something to be ashamed of.

DAY 151 • USE YOUR UNIQUE IMAGINATION

Look around you. Everything you see that is man-made came from the imagination of others. I encourage you to use your unique imagination in all areas of your life. Use your imagination to express yourself, solve problems, and, more importantly, create something new. By bringing together your imagination, life experience, and talents, you give birth to something new through your unique personality. Whatever you create can only come from you, and as a result, you feel alive. This is the joy of creating. What do you want to create?

意味と価値観 Meaning and Value

DAY 152 • OTHERS

As social beings, we find meaning in our relationships and hope we are of value to others. Other people matter, and we hope that we matter to others. Others contribute to our ikigai. We essentially live because of and for others. A common saying in Japan is *Hito wa hitori de wa ikite ikenai*: "A person cannot live alone." While this may not be entirely true, it is very hard to find meaning and value in a life without others. Who would you struggle to live without? Why are these people important to you? How do they give you the feeling of ikigai?

DAY 153 • WORK

To feel ikigai at work, you need a balance of extrinsic factors, such as salary and working conditions, and intrinsic factors, such as work satisfaction—feeling that you're making an impact and growing because of the work you do. Work should be more than just a job; it should be a role that feels meaningful, one that allows you to contribute, grow, and express yourself. List all the intrinsic and extrinsic benefits of your work, and notice what your thoughts and feelings are telling you.

DAY 154 • BELIEF

People with deep religious faith often feel that God or another higher power provides the answers to life's most important questions. Others find meaning in more unconventional beliefs, such as UFOs or the idea that we are living in a simulation. Life is a mystery. Life is challenging. Whatever form it takes, belief can serve as a powerful ikigai source. It can give us a sense of meaning, a reason to keep going, and a way to frame life's struggles within something larger than ourselves. What beliefs help you make sense of life? What feelings do they bring you?

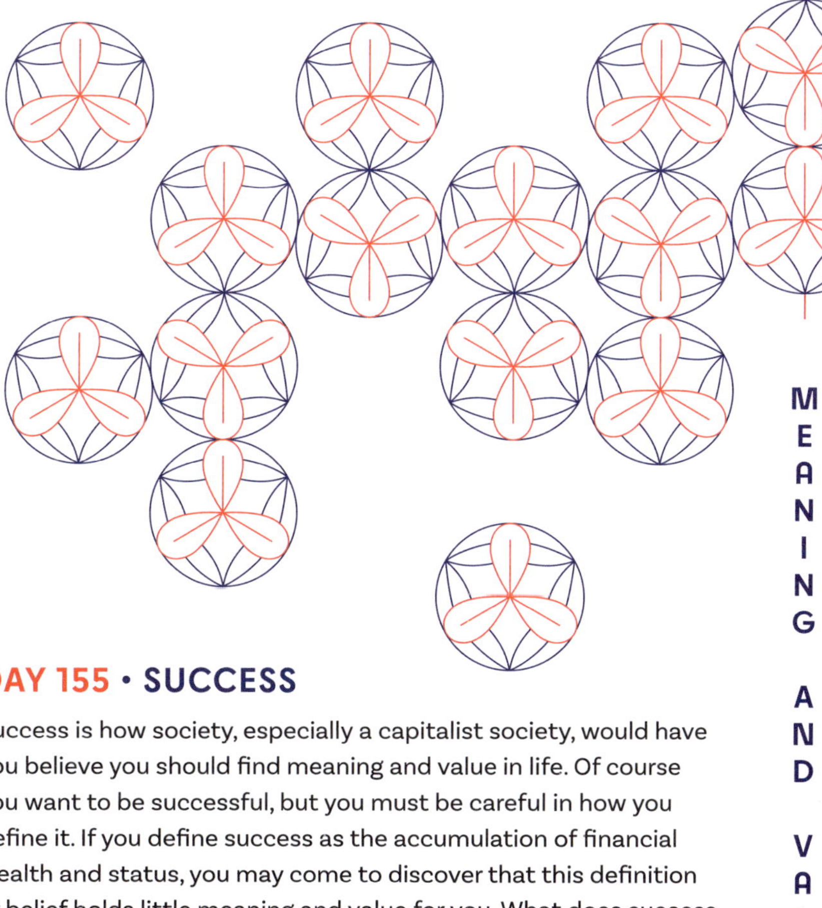

DAY 155 • SUCCESS

Success is how society, especially a capitalist society, would have you believe you should find meaning and value in life. Of course you want to be successful, but you must be careful in how you define it. If you define success as the accumulation of financial wealth and status, you may come to discover that this definition or belief holds little meaning and value for you. What does success look like to you in terms of living a meaningful life?

DAY 156 • SHENANIGANS

If you are like me, you can find meaning and value in shenanigans. We can certainly take life too seriously. Thinking that we must find meaning in all aspects of life can only lead to anxiety. The Japanese proverb *Mitsugo no tamashii hyaku made* (三つ子の魂百まで) tells us that "the soul of a three-year-old remains until one hundred." From time to time, release your inner child and play. Have some fun. Be mischievous. It will make life feel meaningful for you and others.

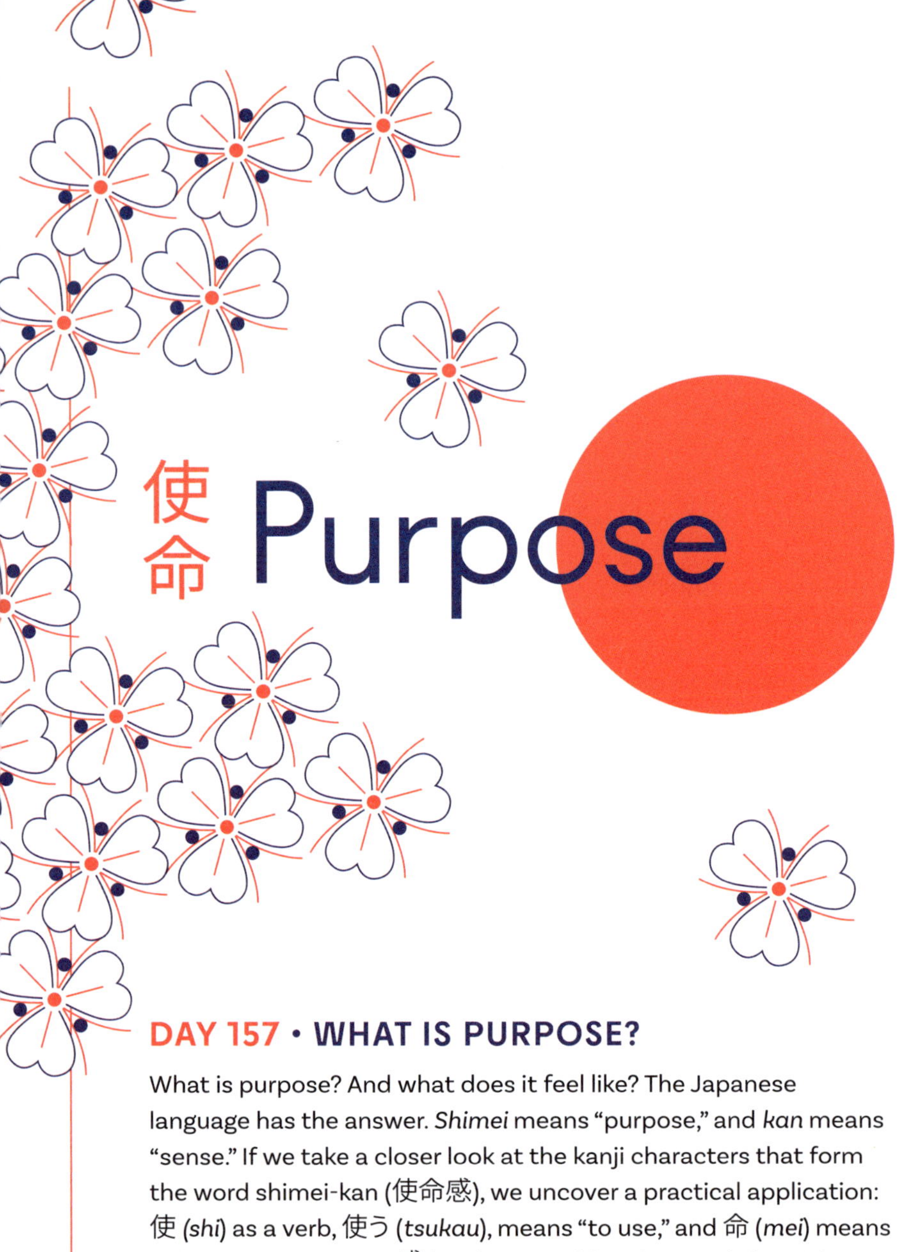

DAY 157 • WHAT IS PURPOSE?

What is purpose? And what does it feel like? The Japanese language has the answer. *Shimei* means "purpose," and *kan* means "sense." If we take a closer look at the kanji characters that form the word shimei-kan (使命感), we uncover a practical application: 使 *(shi)* as a verb, 使う *(tsukau)*, means "to use," and 命 *(mei)* means "life." Thus, along with 感 *(kan)*, we could understand *shimei-kan* as "the feeling of using your life." This is what ikigai feels like. How do you wish to use the life that has been given to you?

DAY 158 • PURPOSE IN THE SMALL

If you can do small things well, then you can do all things well. Finding purpose in the small or the mundane is often trivialized or not valued as worthwhile. In the West, we tend to embrace an all-or-nothing attitude; however, it is a mistake to dismiss the small as unimportant. To do anything well requires a series of steps that must be completed with care. When you do small things well, it means that you care. And when you care, you feel a sense of ikigai. What small things can you do with care to feel a sense of purpose?

DAY 159 • KOKOROZASHI • 志

Imagine a personal mission where you wish to change society—a cause to which you would be willing to commit years, possibly decades. This is *kokorozashi,* and its kanji (志) depicts the heart of a samurai. It comprises two words: *kokoro,* the "heart," "mind," and "spirit" as a single concept, and the verb *sasu,* which means "to point." Together, we could understand kokorozashi to mean "where the heart points" or "where the mind is focused." As such, a kokorozashi comes with an incredible sense of purpose and ikigai. What cause would you be happy to devote your life to?

DAY 160 • FIND YOUR ROLE

Your true purpose in life may be to uncover your unique life role. This means to discover how you want to use your life and pursue it with intention—guided by your values, attuned to your intuition, and committed to doing the work once that role becomes clear. Having a unique role in life to pursue is something we can all achieve; it isn't just reserved for those with wealth or fame. And it doesn't have to be something grand or world-changing—although it certainly can be. Your unique role in life may go unnoticed by others as you quietly fulfill it by serving the people you wish to support.

DAY 161 • BE UNIQUE

Your most important purpose in life is to be you—that is, to be your natural, unique self and pursue what matters to you. Don't listen to others who tell you who you should be. Your dreams and goals may be met with resistance. But the purpose of your life is for you to be your unique self and to pursue what matters to you—your ikigai. Are you holding back from something you want to do or hiding your true self because of others? Give yourself permission to pursue it. Give yourself permission to be yourself.

気 Energy

DAY 162 • O-GENKI DESU KA • お元気ですか

The Japanese greeting *O-genki desu ka* is typically translated as "How are you?" but a more literal translation is "Are you full of energy?" *Ki* refers to the flow of energy within our bodies and the energy we experience and share with others. A person with a strong flow of ki is considered energetic and full of ikigai. In essence, ikigai is what gives you energy. What activities make you feel energized and hungry for life? And who do you feel a strong energy connection with when you're with them?

DAY 163 • YARUKI • やる気

Yaruki is a common Japanese word that literally means "the mindset or heart to do something." It points to a specific task, goal, or challenge that you want to take on because of its intrinsic nature. It's an eagerness to take action on something that will challenge you. Yaruki often uncovers new ikigai sources, as it draws your attention to the things you naturally want to invest your energy in—things you feel are worth doing. What new ikigai source do you want to give your energy to?

DAY 164 • HONKI • 本気

Honki, or "true energy," is the determination to do something even if it comes with a loss. A Japanese friend told me that the ultimate form of honki is a matter of life or death. This statement reminded me of the rock climber Alex Honnold, who in 2017 climbed El Capitan, a 3,000-foot granite wall in Yosemite Valley, without using any ropes or safety gear. One misplaced step, and he would have fallen to his death. Climbing is his ikigai, so the risk was worth it for him. If you are going to pursue your ikigai, do it *honki de*, with true energy.

DAY 165 • NONKI • 呑気

Nonki describes someone who is easygoing, carefree, or happy-go-lucky. Typically, it refers to a homebody who prefers spending time alone rather than going out with friends. They are not driven by goals or success but are instead quite content living a leisurely lifestyle. Nonki reminds us that ikigai doesn't always have to come from doing. It can also arise simply by taking life as it comes, appreciating comfort, and enjoying the present moment more often. Treat yourself to a nonki weekend—just relax and see what ikigai the days bring.

DAY 166 • TANKI WA SONKI • 短期は損気

The Japanese proverb *tanki wa sonki*, meaning "a short temper brings loss," tells us that reacting impulsively or with anger can damage our relationships. Frequent outbursts or temper tantrums directed at those we care about may lead to a loss of ikigai, as we risk hurting the very people who give our lives meaning. A short temper short-circuits your ikigai. Is there someone you've lost your temper with recently? How could you make amends with them? Use your ki—your energy—to reconnect with them.

フロー

Flow

DAY 167 • THE IKIGAI-KAN STATE

Flow is often experienced while playing sports, music, or games. It is generally accepted as an optimal state of mind that is achieved when an individual is intensely involved in one of these activities. But we sometimes forget, as Mihaly Csikszentmihalyi and Isabella Selega Csikszentmihalyi defined, that flow involves a balance between a challenge to be met and the skill level of the individual required to meet it. The benefits of achieving a flow state include high levels of enjoyment and satisfaction, and a sense of fulfillment, all of which we could describe as ikigai-kan. When do you experience flow?

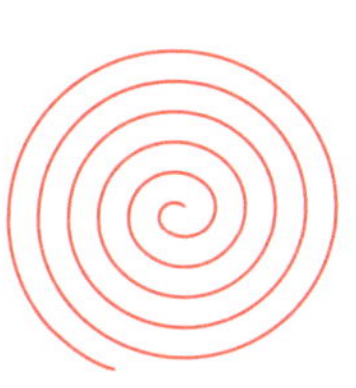

DAY 168 • ICHIGYO-ZANMAI • 一行三昧

Ichigyo-zanmai is a Zen term that translates to "one practice concentration." It is the practice of doing things to the best of one's ability, fully devoting oneself to the task at hand. The power of ichigyo-zanmai is that by limiting yourself to one activity, you simultaneously free yourself to fully express who you are. Doing this doesn't just allow you to feel flow; it also allows you to transmit flow. You become and express flow, capturing it in the work you produce. In this flow state you feel ikigai. What craft or hobby can you fully devote yourself to in order to experience an ikigai flow state?

DAY 169 • CAPTURED FLOW

Captured flow is something we see in the creations of crafts. You may sense this flow when you feel certain artworks call out to you, almost as if the artwork has a soul within itself attempting to communicate with you. This is the ikigai of another resonating with you. I feel this flow when I view Japanese calligraphy on hanging scrolls. Where do you sense captured flow? Visit a museum or gallery this month, or explore artwork online and notice which creations call out to you.

DAY 170 • SOCIAL FLOW

Everywhere you go in Japan, you'll notice customs and practices designed to avoid inconveniencing others. On trains, for example, passengers stay quiet and refrain from private phone calls. These shared behaviors create a culture of social flow and group harmony, giving others the space to enjoy their ikigai. For some Japanese, reading a book on the train might be a small yet meaningful ikigai on their long commute. Where in your life can you be more considerate of others, creating quiet so they can enjoy their ikigai undisturbed?

DAY 171 • FLOWING WATER NEVER SPOILS

Still water becomes stagnant, but water that keeps flowing remains fresh. In the same way, staying engaged in work or study keeps your mind active and your spirit adaptable. Each new challenge or environment becomes an opportunity to learn, stretch, and grow. Like a river that carves its path through shifting landscapes, your journey of ikigai flows forward when you remain open and responsive to change. Life may rush by, but that's far better than drying up like a shrinking puddle. Keep moving, keep learning. This is how we stay alive inside and feel ikigai.

生きがいと心

Ikigai and Your Kokoro

DAY 172 • THE MINDFUL HEART AND THE HEARTFUL MIND

In the West, we believe that you think with the mind and feel with the heart. We separate our logical self and our emotional self as if we should switch from one to the other depending on context or circumstance. In Japanese culture, it is understood that the heart and mind cannot function without being in unison with each other. This is conveyed with the word *kokoro*, the mindful heart and heartful mind that, when in harmony with each other, free your spirit to the moment at hand. This is when you feel ikigai. In what moments do you feel your mind, heart, and spirit come together?

DAY 173 • KOKOROTSUKAI • 心使い

Kokorotsukai literally translates as "use one's heart," meaning to do things for others with consideration, thoughtfulness, or care. Essentially, it means to think compassionately and use your heart when helping someone. It is a source of ikigai when you use your heart to help others because you're expressing compassionate love, which can make someone's life a little easier. Who is someone you know who needs a helping hand with their life right now? Think about what you could do for them and then offer it to them.

DAY 174 • KOKORO-SHIZUKA • 心静か

Ikigai sometimes calls us to experience things with a quiet heart, such as taking the time to slowly sip a drink or quietly complete a chore. As you might expect, the Japanese have a word for this: *kokoro-shizuka*, which means both "a quiet mind" and "a silent heart." Having a quiet mind and a silent heart allows you to notice and experience more ikigai. A quiet heart encourages you to slow down and be still. Where in your life can you do things with kokoro-shizuka?

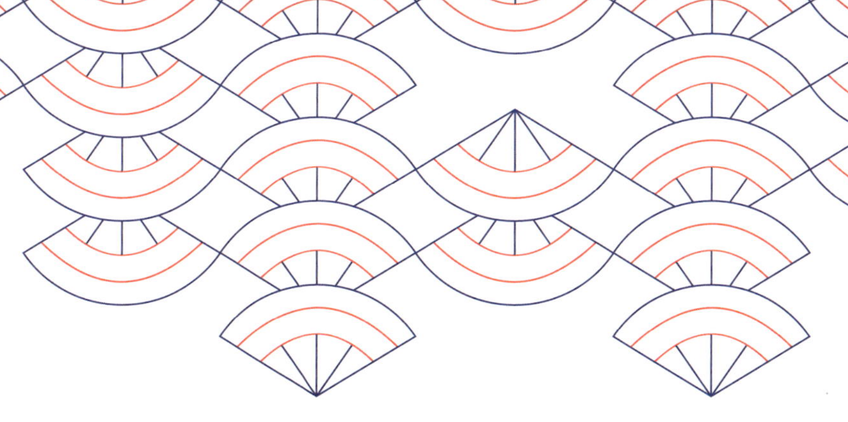

DAY 175 • ZANSHIN • 残心

Zanshin means "the lingering mind," and refers to a mental state in martial arts in which one maintains focus even after completing a strike. It is a crucial aspect of all Japanese martial arts. The spirit of zanshin is equally important in daily life, when you can linger in the moment to fully appreciate it. For instance, after a meal, take time to reflect on and express gratitude for what you have eaten. Ikigai can be felt in the lingering mind. With the spirit of zanshin, practice keeping phones off the table during mealtimes. Notice how presence deepens when you and others are fully engaged in the act of eating and connecting.

DAY 176 • SHOSHIN • 初心

The term *shoshin* is a Zen Buddhist concept that translates to "beginner's mind." It serves as a reminder of the enthusiasm, determination, and humility you have when you first start learning something. The beginner's mind calls us back to the spark of inspiration that ignited our growth and transformation. As we become accustomed to a job, practice, or skill, the mind—often clouded by ego or complacency—can overlook a world of ikigai opportunities. With a beginner's mind, in what familiar activities can you rediscover a spark of inspiration, or that desire to learn and grow?

自然 Nature

DAY 177 • UNIVERSAL SOURCE OF IKIGAI

Nature has so much to offer us, yet we rarely spend time in it. And what a tragedy that is, for spending time in nature opens us up to a world of awe and beauty. It is a universal source of ikigai always available to us. The four-character idiom 花鳥風月 (*kachō fūgetsu*) conveys this idea both practically and poetically, translating to "the beauties of nature" (flower, bird, wind, moon). What beauties of nature can you look forward to experiencing the next time you visit her?

DAY 178 • SAKURA • 桜

Sakura ("cherry blossoms") are valued not only for their delicate beauty but also for their fleeting nature. Despite being translated as cherry blossoms, sakura do not bear fruit; they are not admired for what they produce, but instead for their unique beauty. While they are celebrated when in full bloom, when sakura petals scatter and fall, the Japanese cherish them all the more for their fleeting nature, sensing a unique beauty in their impermanence. Where in your life can you find ikigai in life's beautiful but fleeting moments?

DAY 179 • HANAMI • 花見

Hanami, the viewing of cherry blossoms, is a spring tradition that the Japanese have enjoyed since ancient times. It is essentially picnicking under sakura trees, enjoying food and drinks while admiring the beauty of cherry blossoms in full bloom. The charm of sakura lies not only in their graceful appearance, but also in their soft, sweet fragrance, bringing ikigai to life through simple sensory pleasure. This has led sakura-flavored treats, like sakura mochi, to become popular seasonal delights. How can you celebrate the season you are currently in? Perhaps by preparing a seasonal dish from an inspiring recipe and going on a picnic?

DAY 180 • MOMIJIGARI • 紅葉狩り

Momijigari is the practice of venturing into fields or mountains to enjoy the beauty of autumn leaves. The essence of momijigari lies in immersing oneself in nature to appreciate the vibrant colors of autumn. It serves as a reminder that ikigai can be found in slowing down and simply observing the beauty Mother Nature offers as she transitions through her seasons. How do autumn's colors inspire you?

DAY 181 • KOMOREBI • 木漏れ日

When you visit nature, you may be fortunate enough to witness *komorebi*, or sunlight filtering through the trees. Komorebi can evoke feelings of awe, with soft yet striking sunbeams cutting through the trees, as if God has opened a gateway to paradise. The beauty of komorebi lies in the interplay of light and shadow, forming shifting patterns on the forest floor. This gentle dance reminds us that ikigai, like life, is made of both brightness and shadow. Today, go outside and observe the shadows cast by the sun through nature. Notice what feelings arise as you take in this fleeting beauty.

DAY 182 • YŪGEN • 幽玄

Yūgen is a sense of beauty felt through intuition, imagination, and an appreciation for what is hidden from view in nature. When we admire a sakura tree in full bloom, we see its visible beauty. But it has also endured wind, rain, and snow, and will soon shed its petals. To feel yūgen is to sense the quiet story behind what we see. This is also true for our ikigai—its depth often lies in what others can't see. What unseen experiences, memories, or dreams add depth to your ikigai today?

DAY 183 • MONO NO AWARE • 物の哀れ

Mono no aware, often described as "the pathos of things," captures the profound emotions and subtle melancholy experienced when observing moments of nature, such as the fleeting changes of the seasons. For the Japanese, nature is something that the human heart aligns with and adapts to. Mono no aware is nature's nudge to be mindful of its transient moments. When we are in nature and present to experience such moments of mono no aware, we understand how loss makes life worth living. What loss of an ikigai, a person or constant, has made you appreciate life more? Write the answer in your journal.

NATURE

DAY 184 • FOREST BATHING • 森林浴

In Japanese culture, the relationship between nature and well-being is practiced through *shinrin-yoku* (forest bathing), a term coined in 1982 by the Japanese Ministry of Agriculture, Forestry, and Fisheries. Shinrin-yoku refers to the experience of mindfully being present in and interacting with nature. It is not just simply taking a walk in the woods; it involves engaging all five senses mindfully to fully experience the forest's healing effects. In the case of taste, this could involve drinking pure spring water, tasting edible plants or forest-grown foods, or simply being mindful of the fresh air you breathe.

DAY 185 • SEVENTY-TWO MICRO-SEASONS

The people of Japan, with their love for nature and keen awareness of subtle changes in the natural environment, have identified seventy-two micro-seasons. With each micro-season comes a feeling of ikigai as the Japanese experience the richness and subtleties of nature. Each micro-season is named after the natural changes it reflects, serving as a reminder of the abundance of ikigai found in nature. For example, one micro-season is "first peach blossoms," marking the subtle arrival of spring. What subtle changes in the seasons do you most enjoy? Can you identify your own micro-seasons in the area where you live?

DAY 186 • THE LAND OF THE RISING SUN

As ikigai is often described as what gets you out of bed in the morning, we could say it rises with the sun. In Japan, getting up early to witness the first sunrise of the new year is a deeply meaningful tradition. As the first rays break the horizon, people often pause in awe, reflecting on the past year and making wishes for health, happiness, or growth. In a sense, they are inviting ikigai into the year ahead. Tomorrow morning watch the sunrise while thinking about what ikigai you would like to invite into your life.

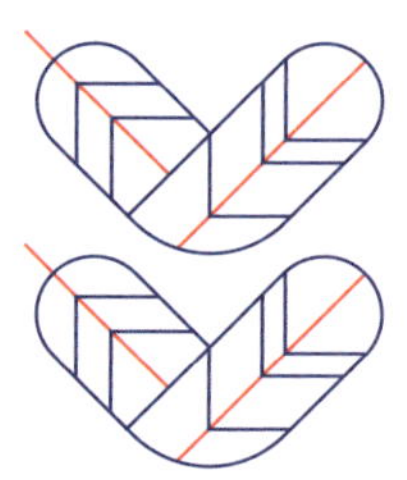

言霊 Kotodama

DAY 187 • WORD SPIRITS

What is it about ikigai that is so appealing? Why has it gained so much fascination and interest in the West? Could it be the word itself has a spirit or soul? Many Japanese believe that words have spirits—a belief known as *kotodama*, with *koto* meaning "language" or "words," and *dama* meaning "soul" or "spirit." We could understand kotodama as a type of "word karma," with the words you regularly use having an influence on your life. If words do carry a spirit, what words could you speak more often to bring ikigai into your life?

DAY 188 • ON • 恩

On carries the meaning of "blessing" or "favor," and is often felt when one recognizes what has been done for them. On encourages you to appreciate the causes that have led to your present state of good fortune. From this perspective, we can see that on is not something we seek out or request; rather, it is something that has already been given to us, even before we asked for it. It reminds us of how much ikigai we already have. In your journal, write in detail about the ikigai and good fortune that currently exist in your life.

DAY 189 • WAKUWAKU • わくわく

Wakuwaku is an onomatopoeia that expresses excitement, anticipation, and joyful energy in response to something fun or enjoyable that's about to happen. It describes a state where your heart races, emotions are stirred, and it's hard to stay still due to excitement. The word comes from the verb *waku*, meaning "to well up," "spring forth," or "gush." In this way, wakuwaku expresses the feeling of joyful anticipation bubbling up inside. Your ikigai often makes you feel wakuwaku. What has you feeling wakuwaku at the moment? If nothing, what would have you feeling wakuwaku?

DAY 190 • MUGAMUCHŪ • 無我夢中

The phrase *mugamuchū* describes a state in which someone is so deeply absorbed in an activity that they forget their current situation or surroundings. We might call this "being in the zone." The term *muga* originates from Buddhist teachings and means to transcend the ego and free oneself from self-centered thoughts, even to the point of forgetting oneself. *Muchū* literally translates as being in the middle of a dream, signifying complete engrossment in something. The spirit of mugamuchū encourages you to immerse yourself completely in an activity to the point where you forget everything else, including your own existence—a state of ikigai flow.

DAY 191 • KIBUN TENKAN • 気分転換

Kibun tenkan means "mood change," a shift from feeling down to feeling more joyful or positive. The spirit of this word encourages you to change things up when you're stressed or low. Small actions like listening to music, eating something sweet, or enjoying a cup of coffee or tea can help shift your mood. These simple practices show that it doesn't take much to move toward a more positive state. When you're feeling stressed or low, how can you call on the spirit of kibun tenkan to bring a little ikigai into your life?

DAY 192 • TSUNDOKU • 積読

Do you love books? Do you have piles of them on your desk, in your home office, or beside your bed? If so, you may be joyfully afflicted with *tsundoku*—the practice of buying books and letting them pile up unread. Tsundoku reflects your curiosity and desire to stay close to ideas that nourish your ikigai. While you may not have time to read them all, simply having books nearby can bring a sense of comfort. They are sources of ikigai patiently waiting for you to make time for them. What books are currently in your tsundoku pile?

DAY 193 • OTSUKARESAMA • お疲れさま

Otsukaresama is a phrase commonly used in everyday conversation to show appreciation for someone's hard work and effort. It translates to "you are tired," but is commonly used to express respect and gratitude for the time and energy others have given throughout the workday. It serves as a gentle reminder of how others have made your day easier and may have directly or indirectly contributed to your sense of ikigai. Who has made your day easier today? Who has given you more space for ikigai? How could you thank them?

DAY 194 • OKAGESAMA • お陰様

Similar to *otsukaresama*, *okagesama* is used to express gratitude for someone's help, kindness, or support. It can also be an exalted way of acknowledging divine or external blessings. The expression translates to "thanks to others," emphasizing that no one is truly self-made. In Japanese culture, it is believed it is essential to live in a spirit of okagesama—with gratitude for all things and all people who help us live. Without them, we wouldn't experience moments of ikigai. In your journal, write about the people, circumstances, or quiet forces that support your life and help you feel ikigai.

DAY 195 • ICHI-GO ICHI-E • 一期一会

Ichi-go refers to "one lifetime," and *ichi-e* means "a single meeting." The term is generally associated with chanoyu, the Japanese way of tea, where each chakai (tea gathering) is understood to be unique—never to be experienced in exactly the same way again, even with the same people. The spirit of this expression reminds us to cherish each encounter as a once-in-a-lifetime moment. It invites us to see every meeting as a moment of ikigai—a chance to bring meaning to life. Reflect and journal about what made a recent social interaction a once-in-a-lifetime moment—one that positively impacted your life and gave it deeper meaning.

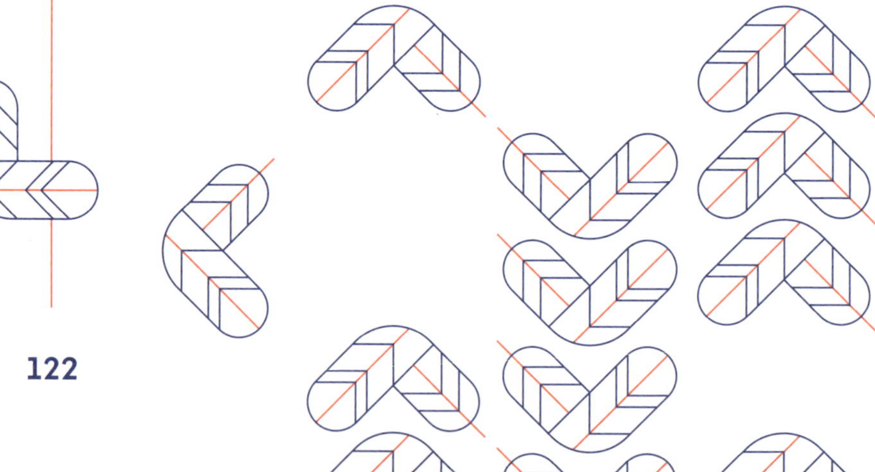

DAY 196 • NICHINICHI KORE KŌJITSU • 日日是好日

The Zen phrase *nichinichi kore kōjitsu* ("every day is a good day") expresses the idea that each day is unique. It reminds us to live each day fully, without dwelling on past regrets or placing excessive expectations on the future. We often judge our days; some feel "good," others "bad," but these are simply perceptions we create. Ultimately, the keys to finding kōjitsu, a good day, are a positive attitude and open mindset. And that, in essence, is ikigai. What small action, mindset, or habit could help you turn today into a kōjitsu—a day worth living?

俳句 Haiku

DAY 197 • HAIKU

Haiku, a short form of poetry, is a unique part of Japanese cultural heritage and a source of ikigai for many who appreciate and compose it. Haiku poems are traditionally composed of three lines with a 5-7-5 syllable pattern, usually capturing a fleeting moment in nature or emotion. Reading haiku brings the vivid imagery of nature and the seasons to life, while often imparting a philosophical life lesson. It can offer a fresh perspective on life, a lens through which to notice the sublime in the everyday—the beauty that is often overlooked yet right in front of us. Challenge yourself to write a haiku poem including a source of ikigai.

DAY 198 • ENERGY AND MEANING

Snow having melted, the whole village overflows with children.
Kobayashi Issa

This poignant haiku reminds us that ikigai often reveals itself in the ordinary rhythms of life. The joy Issa notices isn't found in something miraculous, but in the sight of children rushing outdoors after a long winter. Their play, laughter, and sheer presence fill the village with energy and meaning. This poem reminds us how easily ikigai can be felt in the simple observation of everyday life.

DAY 199 • SILENCE BETWEEN FRIENDS

With one who muses but says not a single word I enjoy the cool.
Hyakuchi

This poem reminds us that silence between friends can transform a shared moment—like the beauty and coolness of an autumn evening—into an ikigai moment. What is obvious need not be stated, for doing so will spoil the moment rather than enriching it. Fortunate is the one who has a friend who knows when to be silent. When can you next resist the urge to state the obvious and instead let the beauty of the moment speak for itself?

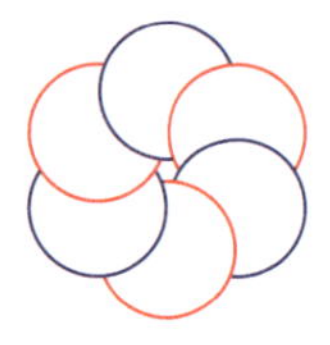

DAY 200 • THE SNAIL

O snail, little by little climb Mount Fuji.
Kobayashi Issa

This haiku tells us that even a tiny snail, by moving at its own pace, can eventually reach the peak of a great mountain. The image of a snail climbing Mount Fuji may seem impossible, yet with steady, patient progress, anything is achievable. The poem reminds us that progress does not need to be rushed. Taking your time allows you to appreciate the journey, find meaning with each step, and foster resilience. How can moving at a steady pace help you nurture more ikigai in the pursuit of your goals?

DAY 201 • SERENDIPITY

A fallen blossom is returning to the branch—look, a butterfly!
Moritake

This poem captures a moment of unexpected beauty. At first glance, the poet sees what appears to be a fallen cherry blossom returning to its branch. But on closer inspection, it's revealed to be a butterfly. The realization of this brief illusion brings not disappointment, but delight, reminding us that ikigai can be felt even in fleeting misconceptions that reveal something unexpectedly beautiful. Where can you find serendipitous moments of beauty in your life?

道 Dō—The Path, The Way

DAY 202 • LIFELONG PURSUITS

Japanese people are enthusiastic learners, with many committing themselves to lifelong pursuits such as *kadō*, flower arrangement; *kodō*, the way of incense; *shodō*, calligraphy; and *bushidō*, the way of the warrior. The suffix *dō* indicates a "way" or a "set of practices" with an emphasis placed on discipline and growth. These practices offer not just skills, but a rhythm and structure to life—something to return to, improve upon, and find joy in. Over time, this kind of dedicated pursuit can become a steady source of ikigai. What personal practice or interest could you begin to treat as your own path, your own dō?

DAY 203 • KADŌ • 花道 THE WAY OF FLOWERS

Kadō is an ancient practice of arranging flowers, branches, moss, and even wild grasses in a vase. Every stem is arranged with precision and care as a way to connect with nature, slow down, and notice beauty in small things. This is what ikigai is all about. You don't need formal training to try it. Even placing a single seasonal flower in a vase can be life-affirming when done with care. What small piece of nature can you bring into your home today to nurture your sense of ikigai?

DAY 204 • KŌDŌ • 香道 THE WAY OF INCENSE

Kōdō is the traditional Japanese art of appreciating the scent of fragrant woods in the form of incense. In kōdō gatherings, participants don't just smell incense, they attune their hearts to subtle aromas that evoke childhood memories, the seasons, and a sense of nostalgic ikigai. This is something you can do, too. Simply lighting incense or pausing to notice a natural scent can bring calm, presence, and connection. What scent takes you back to your past? Can you create a moment today to smell nostalgia and feel ikigai?

DAY 205 • SHODŌ • 書道
THE ART OF CALLIGRAPHY

Shodō is the ancient art of calligraphy, expressing meaning through brush and ink. Traditionally written on hanging scrolls, calligraphy displays words or expressions in homes and tea rooms to invite guests to reflect on the seasons or on life itself. This craft shows how a single word or phrase—like *ichigo-ichie*—can offer meaning and a sense of ikigai when reflected upon. You don't need to be a trained calligrapher to try this. Writing a single word with care can have the same effect. What word or phrase could you write today to inspire a deeper appreciation of life?

DAY 206 • BUSHIDŌ • 武士道
THE WAY OF THE WARRIOR

The term *bushidō* literally means "the Way of the Warrior" and encompasses the moral and ethical principles that samurai were expected to uphold. More than just a system of combat techniques and military strategy, bushidō is often summarized by seven key virtues: justice, courage, compassion, respect, honesty, honor, and loyalty. These values are still present in business culture and personal relationships today, serving as reminders of how to live a life rich in ikigai. Which virtues speak to you? How could you use them to invite more ikigai into your life?

茶の湯

Chanoyu

DAY 207 • TEA GATHERING • 茶会

Chanoyu translates to "hot water for tea" and refers to the ritual of preparing and serving tea at a Japanese tea ceremony. Chanoyu is a quintessential practice of Japanese culture and a source of ikigai for many practitioners. The spirit of chanoyu is often conveyed through four principles: *wa, kei, sei,* and *jaku*—harmony, respect, purity, and tranquility. When embodied, these create a once-in-a-lifetime moment shared by all present at a tea gathering. Yet this is more than a tea philosophy—it can be embraced as a way of life and guide for how to treat others.

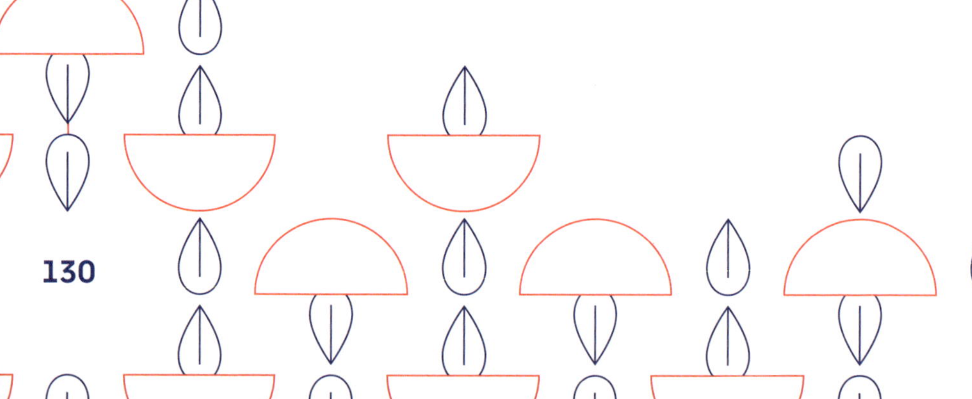

DAY 208 • HARMONY

Harmony is a principle we can integrate into daily life through how we behave and communicate with others. It means seeking synergy, not dominance. Instead of trying to win an argument or push an agenda, we can approach each interaction as an opportunity to build sustainable relationships that benefit everyone involved, now and into the future. Practicing harmony brings a sense of ikigai not only to ourselves but also to those around us. How can you bring more harmony into your life and social world today?

DAY 209 • RESPECT

Respect, a highly prized Japanese cultural value, is something we can offer to all people in our lives. Respectful communication involves not only being polite and thoughtful in what we say but also being quiet and allowing others to speak uninterrupted. With everything we say, we should consider the impact or lasting effect our words have. This is a gift of ikigai we can offer others. How many people can you pay respect to today?

DAY 210 • PURITY

Purity can be applied to our daily routines and habits through a general approach of keeping things in order, maintaining cleanliness of the items we use, and keeping a focused mind while engaging in these activities. We can also cultivate a purity of the mind by questioning our thoughts of judgment, negativity, and hate, and by gently but completely removing these types of destructive thoughts from our minds.

DAY 211 • TRANQUILITY

Tranquility is the result of incorporating harmony, respect, and purity into our lives. The way to cultivate tranquility in our environment is to have fewer material items to worry about and to truly appreciate the items we already own. Whenever possible, we should try to connect our environment to nature. This can be achieved by spending more time in a garden, creating a garden aesthetic, or incorporating the sounds of nature into our home or workplace. Ideas include potted plants, a fountain, or music that features the sounds of nature. How can you bring tranquility into your environment and life?

生きがいの望み

Ikigai Asks You To

DAY 212 • BE PROACTIVE

Due to its experiential nature, ikigai requires action—it calls on you to be proactive. Ikigai won't simply come to you; you uncover it by experimenting, engaging, and learning from life. A proactive life is a life filled with ikigai. A passive life, on the other hand, may let ikigai pass you by. Avoid spending excessive amounts of time on passive activities like watching television or doomscrolling on your phone. List a few things you'd genuinely like to experience in the coming week and approach them with curiosity and presence. Notice which moments make life feel most alive.

DAY 213 • BE CREATIVE

Ikigai wants you to express yourself. You have unique life experiences, unique thoughts, unique ideas, and a unique imagination. Ikigai wants you to express them all in whatever form creativity comes naturally to you. Don't limit your creativity to the artistic. Play with your creativity in all areas of your life. Be creative in your roles, the work that you do, how you communicate, and even your everyday chores. When you express your creativity, you free yourself to play with the world. How can you bring more creativity into your daily life?

DAY 214 • BE PLAYFUL

Ikigai wants you to free your inner child—the playful side you might hide from others outside your family. Let yourself go and be playful when the urge arises. It's something you did naturally as a child, so there's no reason you can't do it now. Be goofy. Sing when you feel like it. Tell bad jokes. Laugh at your own jokes. Make fun of yourself. Life should never be taken too seriously. Ikigai lives in those small, spontaneous moments of light-heartedness. This week, plan something fun with a friend you can goof off with.

DAY 215 • BE AUTHENTIC

As living in alignment is crucial to your ikigai, it serves you to show up as yourself in all of life's interactions. Even when you are challenged, ikigai asks you to speak your truth rather than people-please; to say no when you are being pressured to say yes. For you and your ikigai to flow, speak your mind and follow your kokoro (heart). What is something or someone you are wanting to say no to? Reflect on and write about the reasons for and benefits of saying no.

DAY 216 • BE DILIGENT

With all things worth doing—especially in your interactions with others and in the work you do to serve them—be diligent. Ikigai asks you to communicate with presence and care, and to do even the seemingly inconsequential things with intention and to the best of your ability. It feels good to do things well, to see them through to completion, and to give others your full attention. When you act with care and effort, even small tasks become meaningful, and life becomes richer. Where in your life do you want to show up with more authenticity?

DAY 217 • BE BRAVE

Discovering new ikigai sources may require you to take a leap of faith, embrace uncertainty, and take on new challenges. In order to grow and flourish, we must occasionally step outside our comfort zone and take a risk. Ikigai asks you to believe in yourself and be brave enough to take that first step, because that's what living life to the fullest is all about: feeling the fear and doing it anyway. Overcome a fear this month. Do something that scares you, like rock climbing, public speaking, or signing up for a class you've been hesitant to try.

DAY 218 • BE PATIENT

A purpose-driven ikigai often takes time to take shape and crystallize. You may have only a vague idea of what it is at first, but clarity will come as you take action, learn, and begin to understand what this new ikigai source truly means to you. Just as patience is a virtue that strengthens character, ikigai is a guiding force that gives life direction. Both require presence, intention, and a willingness to stay on the journey. With every step, its clarity as an ikigai source will begin to emerge. Reflect and write about where in your life you need to practice more patience with a meaningful ikigai source.

DAY 219 • BE INCLUSIVE

Ikigai is the spice of life. The more inclusive you are of other people, cultures, and ways of thinking, the more ikigai you uncover, experience, and enjoy. When you open yourself to diverse perspectives and invite others into your social life, your world expands. You gain new insights, build deeper connections, and discover unexpected sources of joy and meaning. These insights may even change your life path. This week, connect with someone from a different background or culture. Ask questions, listen openly, and see where the conversation takes you.

DAY 220 • BE MINDFUL

Be mindful not only of what matters to you, but also of what matters to others. This includes supporting the ikigai of others, but more importantly, it's about being aware of how you interact—what you say, how you listen, and how you use things. An offhand comment, reckless behavior, or ill-timed joke can alienate someone, unintentionally diminish what's important to them, or invalidate their vulnerability. What do you need to be more mindful of in your interactions?

DAY 221 • BE HONEST

For your ikigai to flourish, you must be honest with yourself and others. You must have the personal integrity to pursue what matters to you, rather than feeling obligated to meet the expectations of others. If a role or relationship in your life is not serving you or others well, drains your energy, stifles your creativity, and makes life unpleasant, you need to be honest about it. Ikigai can't be experienced when you're living a lie. What area of your life requires more honesty?

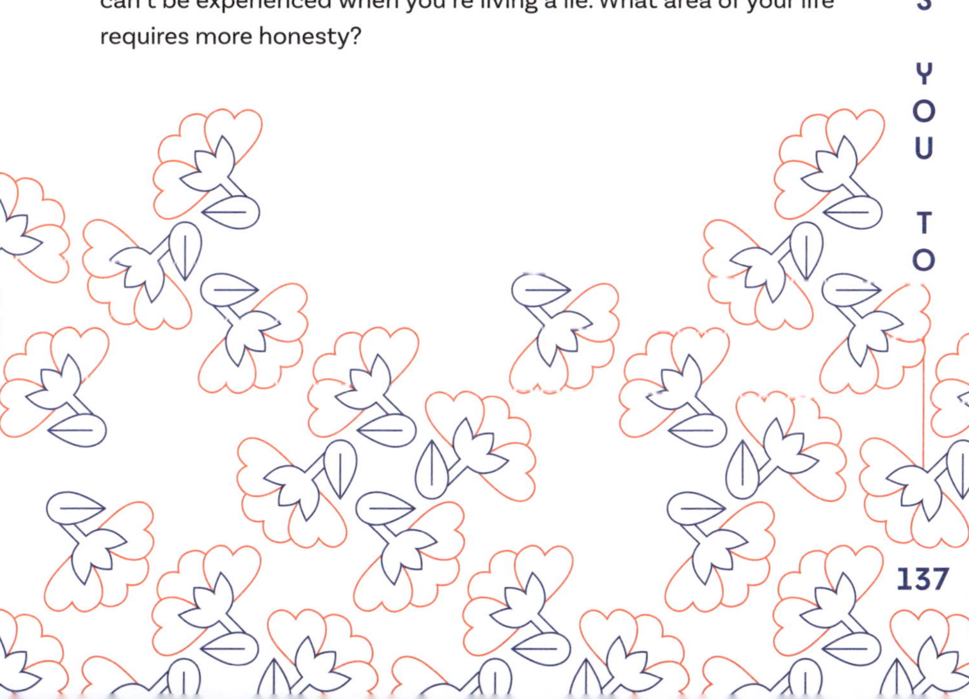

生き甲斐物語

Ikigai Stories

DAY 222 · PERSONAL JOURNEY

Finding what makes life worth living is a deeply personal journey, unique to each individual. Ikigai takes different forms for different people. Over the following days you'll read the voices of many Japanese individuals, from students to retirees—their stories highlight just how varied and personal ikigai can be.

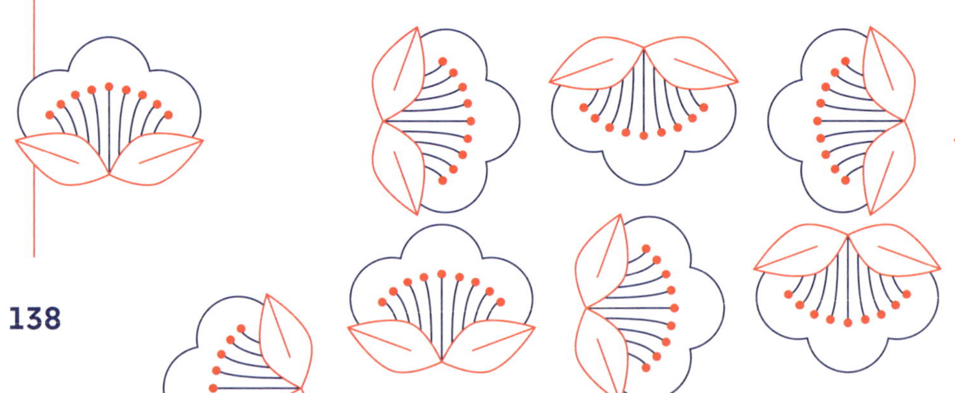

DAY 223 • SUSHI • 寿司

Kanta Kato is a seven-year-old elementary school student. *"My ikigai is enjoying delicious Japanese food. My favorite is sushi, and I especially love tamago (egg) sushi. I feel so happy when I visit a sushi restaurant with my family. For a school project, I interviewed the staff at a sushi restaurant and learned a lot from them. Someday, I want to work in a restaurant and serve delicious food to many people."* Kanta's story reminds us that food isn't just nourishment—it can awaken dreams, spark curiosity, and inspire a sense of purpose rooted in joy, culture, and human connection.

DAY 224 • FOOD: A UNIVERSAL SOURCE OF IKIGAI

Ikigai often reveals itself through the things we're drawn to, and this applies to food as well. For some, it's flavors that delight the senses—for others, it's the stories behind them. Learning about food traditions or engaging with those who craft each dish can deepen our appreciation and open paths to creativity, community, and service. When we explore our interests with curiosity and care, even something simple like a favorite meal can grow into a meaningful journey. Whether you love cooking, eating, or discovering new dishes, your connection with food might just be the start of something deeper. What has a favorite food experience taught you lately?

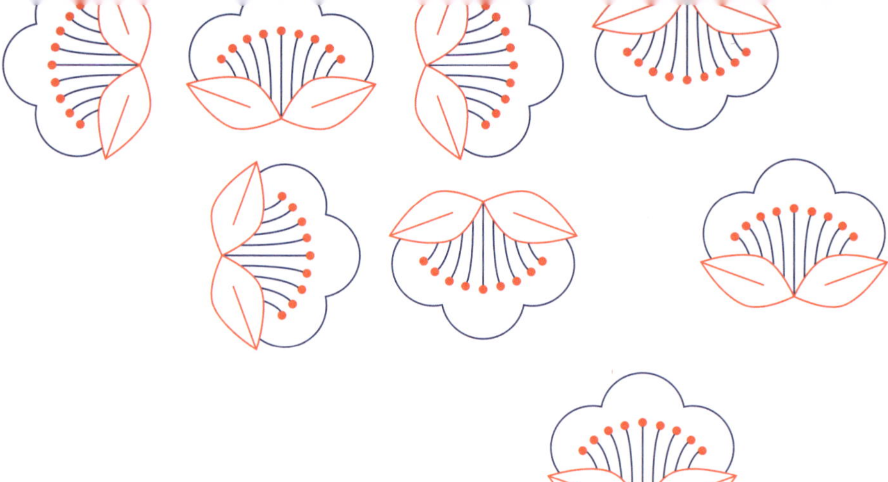

DAY 225 • CREATING SOMETHING

Genki Kato is a twelve-year-old middle school student. *"I feel ikigai when I create something. For example, I enjoy making video games using my computer. I've learned programming to do this. While learning new things can be challenging for me at times, it makes my life richer and gives me a sense of satisfaction. I feel especially happy when my family and friends play and enjoy the games I've made—it's what makes me feel ikigai."* Genki's ikigai highlights how creativity fused with perseverance becomes deeply fulfilling. When passion fuels learning and personal growth, the process itself becomes as meaningful as the outcome.

DAY 226 • SHARING OUR SKILLS

Ikigai often comes from the effort we put into cultivating skills and acquiring new knowledge, which we then use to express our creativity. When we share the fruits of our labor with others, this act itself also becomes a source of ikigai. Using your unique imagination to create something new results in a living expression of your life and validation that you are unique and have something to offer others. How do your unique skills contribute to your purpose? In what ways does sharing your skills deepen your ikigai?

DAY 227 • BELONGING

Ai Nakamura is a twenty-year-old university student and restaurant worker. *"My ikigai is spending time with my mom—especially going out together to browse cute clothes or homeware, and watching live concerts of the artists she loves. There's no one else who shares my taste or understands me the way my mom does. That's why being with her feels like my ibasho—the place where I feel most excited and comfortable."* Ai's story shows how ikigai can be found in everyday moments of connection. When someone feels like your ibasho, it means they truly see you—and that bond becomes a source of joy and belonging.

DAY 228 • SHARING WITH FAMILY

A close relationship with a parent or family member is a wonderful source of ikigai, especially when traditional roles give way to genuine friendship. Since family, especially parents, tend to understand us more intimately, spending time together creates a safe space where everyone can be themselves. For Ai, these shared moments may also be a way of giving back to her mom. How would you like to give back to your parents or family? This week, spend an afternoon or evening with a parent or family member and take them out to do something they enjoy. Do this not out of duty, but because you want to.

DAY 229 • FORZA FERRARI

Jun Hayashi is a twenty-one-year-old musician and game developer. *"My ikigai is watching F1. I feel ikigai when my favorite team, Ferrari, wins. When Ferrari wins, in that moment it's the only thing that matters to me. The frustration I feel when they lose makes me wish I didn't support them at all, but I soon become hopeful and look forward to the next race."* Jun's story shows how ikigai can arise from passion-fueled loyalty. The highs and lows of being a fan reflect our emotional investment—and how resilience and hope can flourish even in the face of defeat.

DAY 230 • SPECTATORSHIP

Supporting a sports team is a powerful source of ikigai—one that brings deep emotional engagement. For Jun, each Ferrari race is a rollercoaster of anticipation, joy, or heartbreak. Sports awaken our raw emotions and connect us to a shared community of fans across the world. These highs and lows aren't just entertainment—they remind us that caring deeply is part of being human. Whether it's through chants in a stadium or quiet cheers at home, spectatorship creates memories that stay with us. Which team or player has made your heart race, and why do you keep coming back?

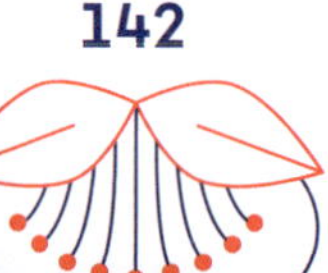

DAY 231 • CONCERTGOING

Momo Suzuki is a twenty-two-year-old university student. *"My ikigai is going to idol concerts. Being in the special atmosphere of a live show, separate from everyday life, helps me forget daily worries, anxieties, and stress. From the bottom of my heart, I can enjoy the music and dancing—it enriches my life."* Momo's ikigai reminds us how stepping into a moment of pure joy can renew us. Live performances offer more than entertainment—they become emotional sanctuaries where the music, the movement, and the crowd's energy combine to lift our spirits and remind us of what makes life beautiful.

DAY 232 • ADMIRATION

Ikigai can be sparked by admiration—especially when we witness someone fully immersed in their craft. Concerts heighten awareness and joy, offering a form of *collective ikigai* where thousands share a love for music or an artist. The feeling of being "seen" by someone we admire creates a moment that lingers long after the show ends. But admiration goes deeper than fandom—it can ignite passions, provide understanding, and inspire us to dream. Artists remind us that creativity is a lifeline. Think of someone whose artistry moves you. What does it awaken in you? How might that spark ripple through your own life?

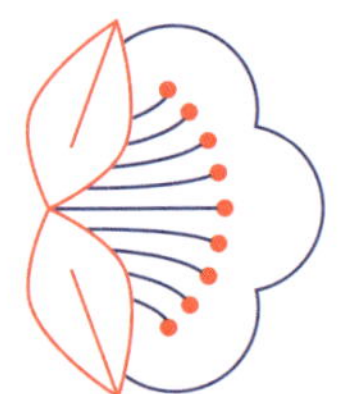
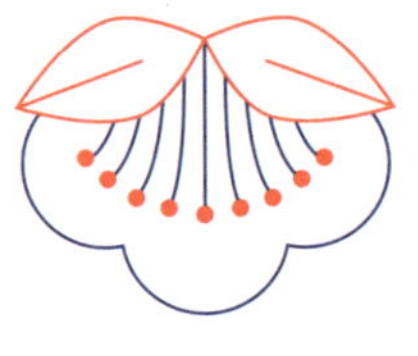
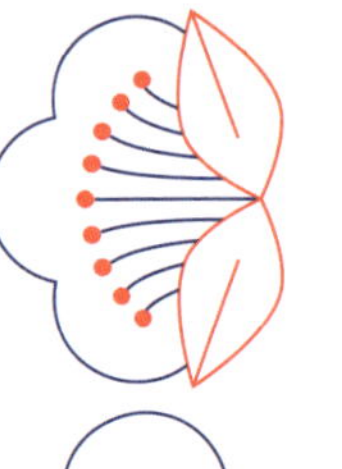

DAY 233 • NEW WORLDS

Kako Shimonishi is a twenty-eight-year-old international student studying in Australia. *"My ikigai is traveling. No matter how much my surroundings have changed—whether I'm an international student abroad or living in Japan—my ikigai has remained constant. I love seeking new experiences and discovering places I've never seen before. I am deeply inspired by my ikigai, which opens doors to new worlds."* Kako's ikigai reminds us that ikigai can be uncovered in new places and through the new experiences that come with travel. These experiences result in personal growth, a stronger sense of self, and more ikigai to enjoy.

DAY 234 • AGENCY

A crucial factor in feeling ikigai is agency. Ikigai often begins with self-awareness—but it flourishes through agency. Having the freedom to make your own choices and live life according to your instincts and values is when you'll feel you are walking the ikigai path. Agency means making meaningful choices and taking ownership of your direction. Ikigai becomes real when, after identifying what matters most, you take action and begin living the way you truly want to. Kako's story reflects this beautifully. Her desire to seek new experiences and discover new places, whether she's home in Japan or a student in Australia, shows she is walking her ikigai path. What choices and journeys do you want to take to walk your ikigai path?

DAY 235 • SPENDING TIME WITH MY FRIENDS

Reina Sano is a twenty-two-year-old PhD student in psychology. *"My ikigai is spending time with my friends. Driving, traveling, or eating out with them makes both me and my life happier. The moments when we joke around and laugh together help me forget any stress or bad feelings. I also like taking photos to capture those moments, so I can look back on them later and feel more motivated to keep going."* Reina's ikigai shows how joy shared with friends can lighten the weight of everyday life. In laughter, adventure, and snapshots, we create memories that help us move forward.

DAY 236 • FRIENDSHIP

Ikigai can come from connection—not just deep talks, but the laughter and spontaneity that friends bring. Driving, traveling, eating—these everyday things feel special when shared with friends. Sometimes, friends offer what even family can't: a space to laugh, be yourself, and let go. As Reina shared, these moments help her forget stress and recharge. It's no surprise she wants to capture them and relive those good times. The feeling of friendship reminds us we don't have to navigate life alone and can make life feel worth living. Which friend would you like to catch up with? Reach out to them and make a date to spend time together.

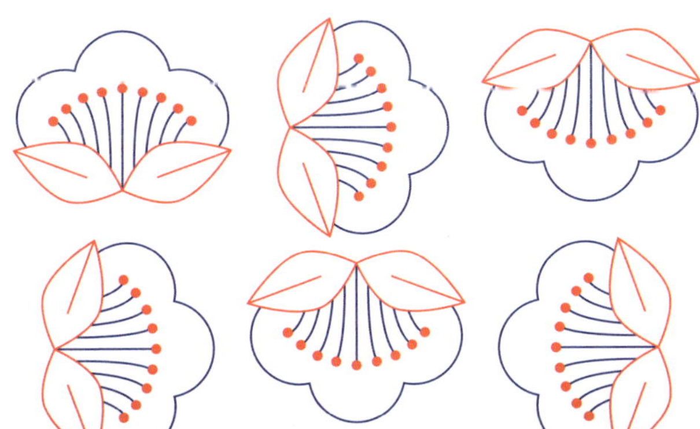

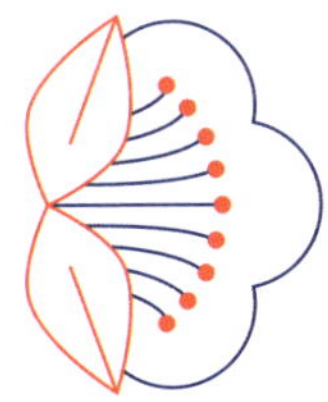

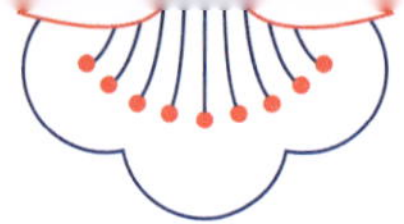

DAY 237 • DISNEYLAND

Maya Matsui is a twenty-three-year-old PhD student in psychology. *"My ikigai is going to Disneyland. Disneyland brings me so much joy, and I always have an incredibly fun time. I love going because there's so much to do—admiring the beautiful scenery, eating delicious food, riding attractions, meeting characters, and shopping for all kinds of merchandise."* For Maya, Disneyland isn't just a theme park—it's a vibrant tapestry of experiences, a place where happiness multiplies. In every corner and encounter, she finds delight, proving that ikigai can live in the heart of fantasy.

DAY 238 • ESCAPISM

Ikigai can be a place or a state of mind—somewhere you go to forget the worries and concerns of daily life and simply enjoy yourself. For Maya, that place is Disneyland: a world of fantasy and adventure offering both novelty and comfort, making it deeply special to her. In this sense, we might say that ikigai, when tied to a place like Disneyland, can also be a form of joyful escapism. Where do you like to escape to in order to feel ikigai?

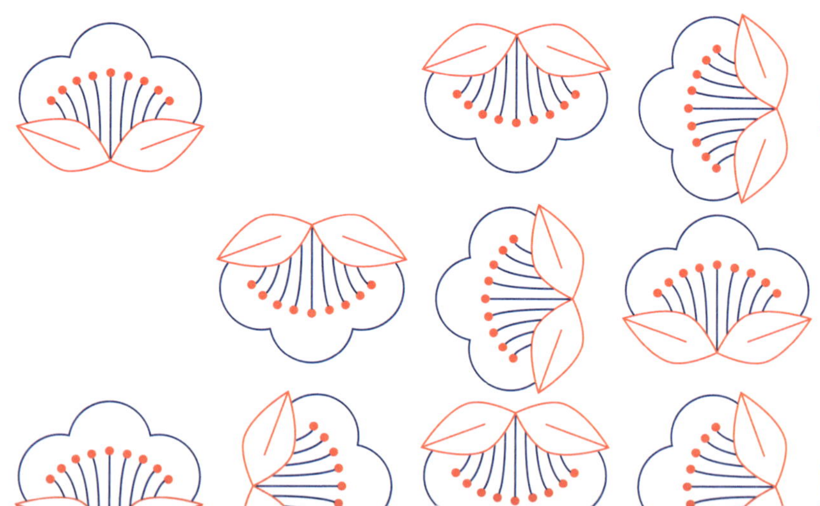

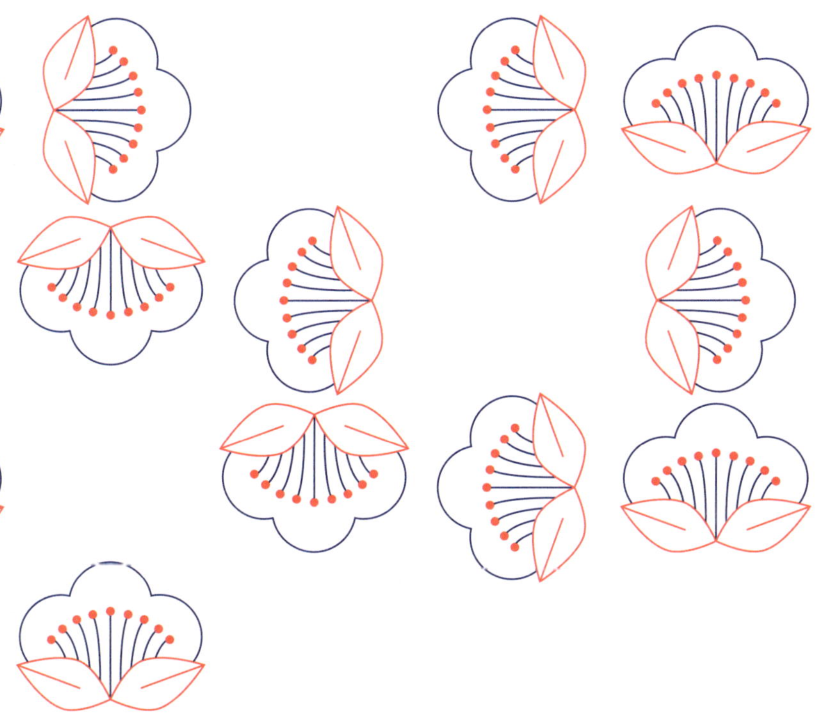

DAY 239 • PLAYING MUSIC

Fuka Itō is a twenty-three-year-old aspiring musician and graduate student. *"My ikigai is playing instruments and listening to music. When I'm immersed in music, I feel fulfilled. Playing or listening to music with someone else creates a connection that can't always be felt through words alone."* As Fuka shares, playing or simply listening to music creates a connection that goes beyond words. Music is a universal source of ikigai that speaks straight to the heart.

DAY 240 • CREATIVE INTIMACY

A creative pursuit like playing music can fill life with meaning and joy, where a type of creative intimacy can be deeply felt. A familiar song can bring comfort, lift your spirits, and change the mood of your day. How can you bring more music into your life? What piece of music would lift your spirits and make you feel joy today?

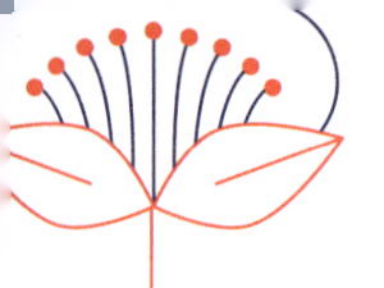

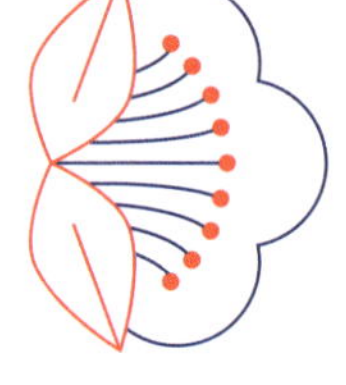
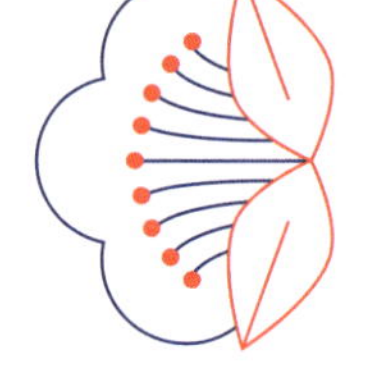

DAY 241 • MARO

Shiori Jonokuchi is a twenty-three-year-old PhD student in psychology. *"My ikigai is spending time with my pet, Maro, a cheeky little Yorkshire Terrier. I adopted him as a puppy during COVID and have been watching him grow ever since. Whenever I'm going through a hard time, he stays right beside me. Just having him near helps me feel better."* For Shiori, ikigai comes on four paws and a wagging tail. Maro isn't just a pet—he's a constant companion, a quiet healer who helps her through hard times with unconditional presence. In Maro, she finds comfort and joy.

DAY 242 • PETS

Pets are a common source of ikigai in Japan—and it's easy to see why. They are loyal, playful, and nonjudgmental companions who offer comfort and protection. There's the joyful tail-wagging of a dog or the soft purr of a cat curled on your lap. They seem to sense when we're feeling down and stay close, offering quiet support. Pets are family. They help turn a house into a home, which is why losing them can be so deeply painful. How have your pets or animals made you feel needed and loved?

DAY 243 • OSHIKATSU • 推し活

Kana Kato is a twenty-three-year-old PHD student majoring in psychology. *"My ikigai is oshikatsu, supporting the artists I love. Whether I'm listening to my favorite songs or going to see musicals, doing these activities helps me forget the busyness of daily life. It also gives me something to look forward to and motivates me to get through each day."* *Oshikatsu* (推し活) is more than fandom—it's a popular and meaningful term in modern Japanese culture that refers to idolization or "supporting your favorite," whether that's a pop idol, anime character, sports player, or even a brand or fictional world. For Kana, devotion to beloved performers isn't just a hobby—it's her ikigai. Through music, theater, and the joy of shared admiration, she finds a steady rhythm of inspiration and emotional uplift.

DAY 244 • IDOLIZATION

Oshikatsi is similar to being a die hard fan but involves a more intentional, respectful, and often ritualistic practice of support rather than being loud and boastful. When we admire others, they give us hope and often inspire us to live with more passion. Like Kana, many find motivation in their support—a spark that brightens routine and renews purpose. In this way, oshikatsu becomes a source of both inspiration and ikigai. Who do you admire so deeply that supporting them gives you energy?

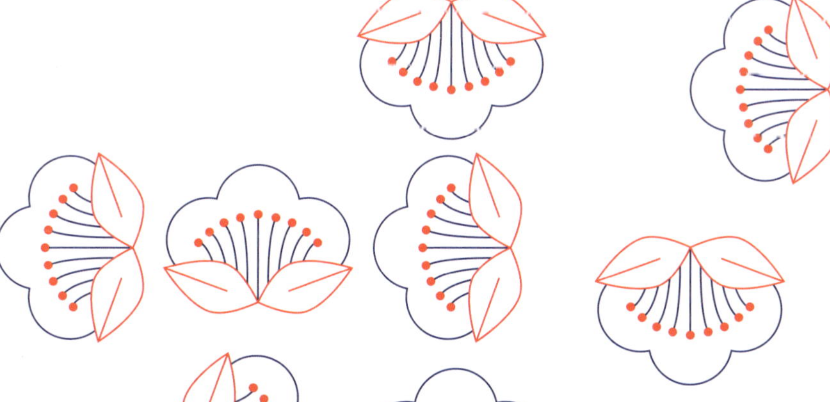

DAY 245 • WAKING UP EXCITED EACH DAY

Minako Horaguchi is a forty-four-year-old ikigai coach and NLP practitioner. *"My ikigai is helping people discover and live their unique purpose with greater ease and peace. I wake up excited for each new day—people, nature, and small moments fuel my spirit and keep me inspired. Engaging with my own ikigai helps me focus on what truly matters, day by day. Honestly, living ikigai isn't always sunshine. Sometimes I feel stuck or useless. When that happens, I try to be kind to myself, sleep on it, and trust that the next morning will feel like a brand-new beginning."* Two words stand out in Minako's reflection: peace and ease. Her story reminds us that ikigai isn't about perfection—it's about showing up for life with gentleness, even on hard days. When we pursue purpose with compassion and presence, we begin to notice the small moments that nourish us and make each day worth waking up for.

DAY 246 • SELF-KINDNESS

As Minako points out, when ikigai is tied to purpose, it's not always sunshine. We can feel stuck or even useless in our roles or while pursuing our goals—especially when our ikigai involves helping others. A sense of social obligation can create pressure and emotional fatigue. That's when it's time to pause, take stock, and extend the same kindness to yourself that you offer to others. Give yourself space to rest, recharge, and trust that a new day will bring renewed clarity and energy.

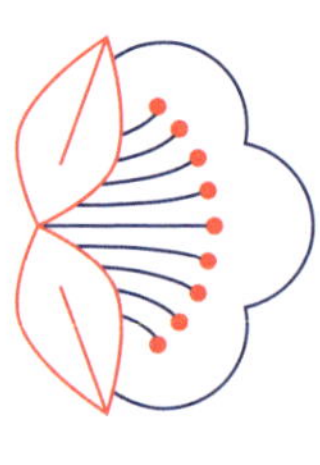

DAY 247 • EVERYDAY MOMENTS

Keiko Yamada is a thirty-four-year-old founder of a wellness company. *"My ikigai is found in everyday moments that bring joy to my soul—phone calls with my family abroad, meaningful conversations with my husband, uncontrollable laughter with friends, and taking a hot bath after a long day."* Keiko's ikigai reminds us that it is often experienced in the company of others—what Japan's Health and Ikigai Advisors call Second-Person Ikigai. Both the people and the shared experiences become sources of ikigai, making the time spent together deeply nourishing to the soul.

DAY 248 • WHAT NOURISHES THE SOUL

Ikigai is what nourishes the soul—what makes you feel connected and sustains your sense of meaning, joy, and inner vitality. It can come through connection with others or simple self-care practices, like taking a hot bath. The beauty of ikigai is that it doesn't require much. For Keiko, it's a phone call to family, a meaningful conversation with someone she loves, shared laughter with friends, or a quiet soak at the end of the day. What are the moments that nourish your soul?

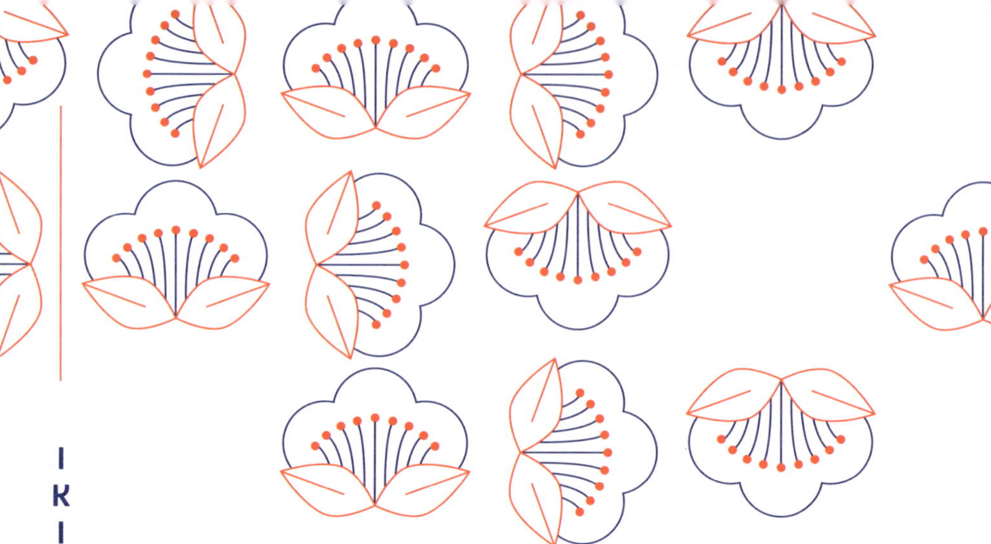

DAY 249 • WALKING

Rino Sekijima is a twenty-three-year-old university student and part-time hotel worker. *"My ikigai is taking walks alone. On the way home from uni or walking from the nearest station to my house, when I walk alone while looking at the scenery, I feel a real sense of being alive. I really enjoy the feeling of my feet touching the ground and the wind blowing against me. As I walk, I'm able to feel grateful just for the ability to walk."* Rino's quiet walks show how ikigai can come from reconnecting with the body. Each step becomes a rhythm of noticing—returning us to ourselves, without rush.

DAY 250 • SLOWING DOWN

Rino's ikigai is a beautiful reminder of how ikigai-kan can be felt in the small, everyday actions we often take for granted. When we slow down and tune in to these moments, we begin to notice the subtle yet powerful sensations that come with them, like the feeling of our feet on the ground or the breeze on our skin. Ikigai is all around us, woven into the fabric of daily life. To experience it, we simply need to be present. Even something as simple as walking can become a source of ikigai worth appreciating. What everyday actions could you learn to appreciate more?

DAY 251 • CHILDREN

Miyuki Imaeda is a twenty-four-year old mother of two and aspiring professional. *"My ikigai are my children. Spending time with them is the most precious part of my life. Especially when I see their sleeping faces at the end of the day, I feel there's nothing in the world that could replace that moment. It's a feeling that softens me completely, and I find myself smiling without even realizing it."* Miyuki's reflection shows how parenting can shift the way we experience time. Those quiet nighttime moments become a gentle reward—a reminder of how love accumulates in the ordinary rhythm of daily life.

DAY 252 • OUR ROLES AND CONNECTIONS WITH OTHERS

Ikigai is deeply tied to our roles and our connections with others, and few bonds are stronger than that between parent and child. As Miyuki shared, spending time with her children is the most precious part of her life. You know you're feeling ikigai when simply looking at a loved one makes you smile. Still, it's easy to take family and those closest to us for granted. The key message here? Spend more time with the people you love—especially family. Who brings a smile to your face? Can you find some time today to be with them?

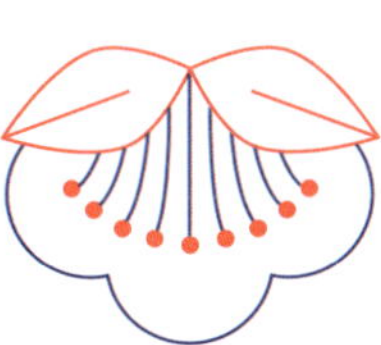

DAY 253 • WHAT FILLS YOU WITH ENERGY

Chiharu Nakayama is a twenty-four-year-old graduate student studying psychology and a music lover. *"My ikigai is going to live concerts of my favorite artists. When I purchase a ticket or a concert date is set, I feel motivated to work hard leading up to it. Attending a concert fills me with energy and brings a big smile to my face."* Chiharu's experience reminds us that ikigai isn't always about the event itself—it's also about what it fuels in us. The anticipation gives her a surge of purpose, and the experience recharges her spirit. Energy and ikigai often go hand-in-hand, turning joy into momentum for everything else.

DAY 254 • WHAT RECHARGES YOU

Ikigai is often tied to the things that energize us—not just emotionally, but physically and mentally. It might be a concert, a creative outlet, a morning routine, or spending time with certain people. When something fills us with energy, we feel more capable, optimistic, and alive. Chiharu's concerts light that spark for her, but energy looks different for everyone. The key is recognizing what lifts you up, and inviting it into your life more often. What activity or ritual helps you reset, re-center, and rise with renewed energy?

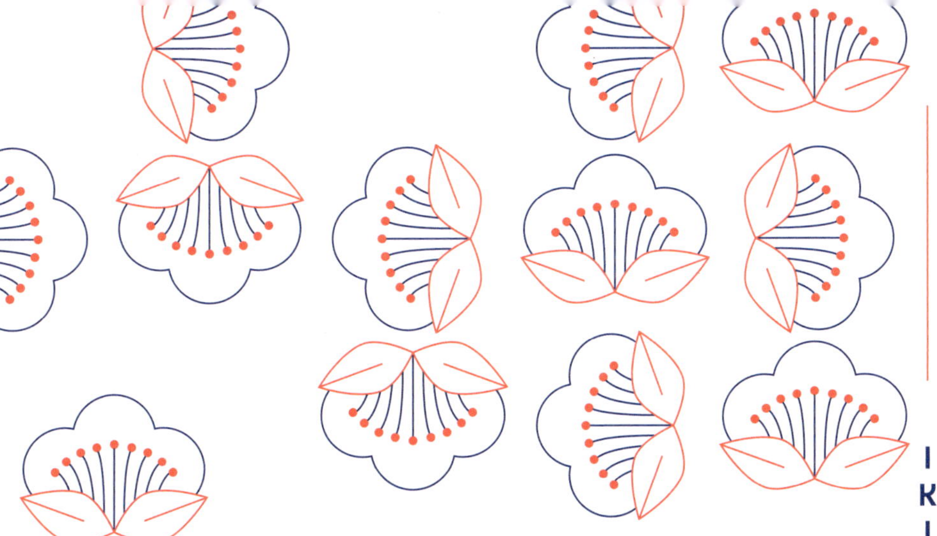

DAY 255 • ALONE TIME

Misaki Endo is a twenty-five-year-old retail and marketing assistant. *"My ikigai is spending time by myself, exploring Spotify playlists, and being with my favorite people. For me, alone time is essential. Stepping back from the outside world and spending time with myself feels comforting, helps me reset my mind, and gives me the motivation to keep going."* Misaki's words remind us that creating space for ourselves can become a quiet kind of strength. When we're alone, we become more attuned to our energy—how we feel, what we need, and what truly restores us. Ikigai doesn't always arrive with excitement; sometimes, it whispers in stillness.

DAY 256 • TIME

Time is our most precious resource. Taking care of it by relaxing, listening to music, or simply sleeping can create a calming sense of ikigai. It's that feeling of *yutori*, spaciousness, that we all need in today's hyper-busy world. As Misaki shared, stepping back from the outside world and spending time alone helps reset the mind and renew motivation. How can you better care for your time? In what ways can you rest to feel more ikigai and stay inspired?

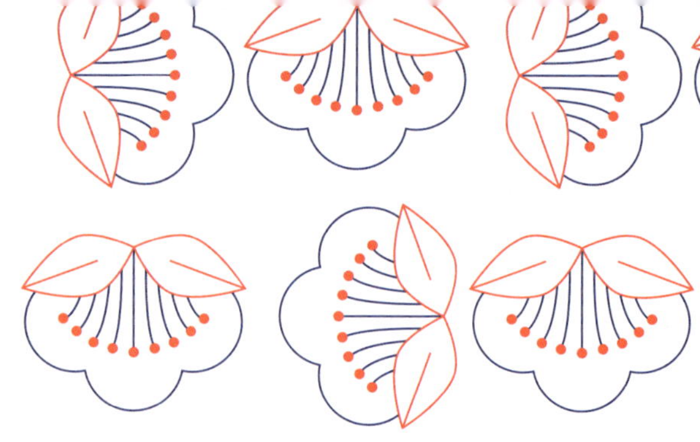

DAY 257 • WHEN I'VE HAD A GREAT DAY

Tamaki Nishimura is a twenty-eight-year-old mother of three and an entrepreneur. *"My ikigai is that moment when I know I've had a great day and can fall asleep feeling accomplished. It's the satisfaction of successfully completing a project at work, the exhilaration of finishing a triathlon, or simply the joy of spending an entire day playing with my kids, then collapsing into the futon with them. I feel worn out but happy."* Tamaki's ikigai is stitched together by motion, effort, and heart. Great days don't just happen—they're built through action and presence. True fulfillment often comes when we've poured ourselves fully into life and feel content in the tiredness that follows.

DAY 258 • ACTIVITIES THAT FULLY ENGAGE US

Ikigai often arises from proactive behavior. Each day is a fresh opportunity to create ikigai-kan—feelings of satisfaction, exhilaration, joy, and accomplishment. Whether it's completing a challenging project, achieving a personal goal, or sharing meaningful moments with loved ones, ikigai often comes from activities that fully engage our skills, energy, and attention. Meaningful activities reminds us that ikigai can be found in experiences that leave us feeling enriched, content, and maybe even exhausted.

DAY 259 • THE COMFORT OF A PARTNER

Ayumi Umeda is a thirty-one-year-old university professor, researcher, and clinical psychologist. *"Spending time with my husband is my ikigai. Being with him gives me a sense of safety, positivity, and boosts my self-esteem. Even when daily life gets tough, I feel like I can manage as long as we're together. I am very satisfied with my life because he is by my side, and I feel truly fulfilled."* Ayumi's story reminds us that ikigai isn't always found in doing—it's found in being. The presence of someone who lifts us up can shape how we face each day. Sometimes, love itself is the energy we need to feel whole.

DAY 260 • YOUR LIFE PARTNER

As Ayumi expresses, the presence of her husband gives her strength, self-worth, and a sense of fulfillment. Without such connection, life can feel incomplete. But with someone to share life with, we are reminded that we were not born to live alone. A life partner is more than just a companion—they can be a deep and lasting source of ikigai. With someone by our side, we feel seen, supported, and safe enough to face life's challenges. Like all good things in life, ikigai is richest when shared. What does emotional safety in a relationship feel like for you?

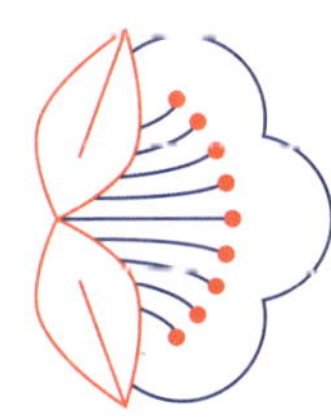

DAY 261 • A PARENT'S IKIGAI

Shintaro Kono is a thirty-four-year-old father, gamer, and university professor who lives in Canada. *"Researching and teaching the connection between leisure and well-being, including the concept of ikigai, helps me feel a sense of ikigai. But, most importantly, as a new dad, I like to hold my newborn son and take care of him. The connection between a parent and a child and the feeling of being needed have become special sources of my ikigai."* Becoming a parent doesn't just shift priorities—it can awaken a deeper sense of purpose. In Shintaro's gentle moments of care, we glimpse an emotional core of ikigai: the joy of presence, the gift of being needed, and the quiet power of connection.

DAY 262 • FEELING NEEDED

Shintaro's offering is a fine example of how a new role can become a life-affirming source of ikigai. The simple yet loving act of holding his son makes life worth living for him. This highlights how ikigai is very much tied to family or our social world and is experienced or felt intensely from giving care and sharing intimacy. Connection and feeling needed are two strong indicators of ikigai, often mentioned as psychometric items in scales that measure ikigai. How has stepping into a new role—like parent, caregiver, mentor, or partner—reshaped how you experience ikigai?

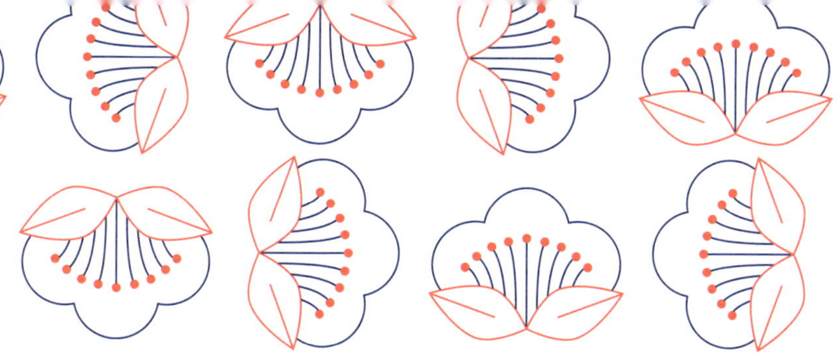

DAY 263 • CONVERSATIONS

Andriana Ubunuki-Kalfa is a fifty-one-year-old performance and executive coach for leaders and athletes. *"For me, ikigai is enjoying a deep, unhurried conversation with someone dear. These moments remind me of what matters most. They bring calm and perspective. Connecting through honest talks makes me feel grateful and motivated at the same time. That is why I made meaningful dialogue my life's work."* Conversations don't just spark ideas—they affirm our place in someone else's life. Andriana's experience reveals how being present, listening, and offering insight can foster mutual growth. When we help others uncover something within themselves, we feel needed. In that moment, our existence feels purposeful and deeply connected.

DAY 264 • TRANSFORMATIVE DIALOGUE

Ikigai is deeply rooted in social connection and the feeling of being understood. One of the most powerful ways we connect is through meaningful dialogue—offering the gift of space for someone to speak while we listen intently. When we receive this gift, a single conversation can be transformational, altering the course of our lives. Can you recall a conversation that positively shaped your path? Have you ever thanked the person who sparked that change?

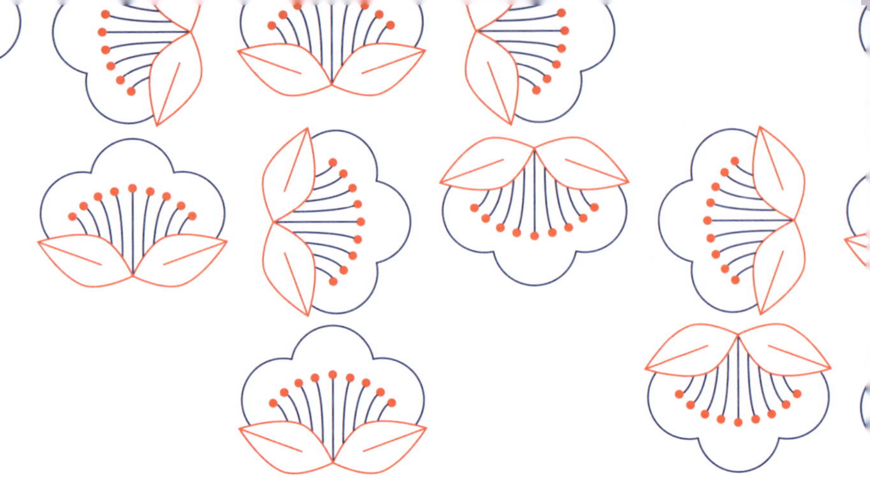

DAY 265 • TEACHING

Daiki Kato is a forty-four-year-old university professor. *"I have many sources of ikigai in my life. One of the most fulfilling is my work teaching psychology to my students and collaborating with them on research. For me, ikigai is deeply tied to the sense of connection and communication I share with my students—it's something I truly value."* For Daiki, not only is teaching psychology to his students fulfilling, but collaborating with them on research is something he truly values. This indicates that teaching is not just the transfer of knowledge but also an intimate, intellectual, and at times emotional process between the student and teacher, where connection results from communication.

DAY 266 • CONNECTION AND COMMUNICATION

We all have opportunities to decide what we'd like to pass on to others, but true connection often emerges when we collaborate. In working side-by-side—whether on research, creative projects, or shared goals—we not only exchange knowledge, but also affirm each other's value. Collaboration can awaken a sense of being needed and trusted, turning the act of sharing into something transformational. Who would you like to collaborate with? What knowledge would you like to uncover and share together?

DAY 267 • A VIRTUOUS CYCLE

Yu Kanazawa is a thirty-six-year-old researcher who studies emotions, psychology, philosophy, and language education. *"My ikigai lies in the virtuous cycle of reading, researching, thinking, and teaching. My research is intrinsically tied to education. Applying theoretical findings in my teaching and gaining insights from students not only enhances pedagogical effectiveness but also contributes to the iterative process of refining academic inquiry. This dynamic interplay between research and practice is both intellectually stimulating and deeply fulfilling."* Yu's practice shows how learning and teaching fuel each other in a loop of growth. Beyond sharing knowledge, this cycle is driven by curiosity and reflection. In that exchange, we don't just teach—we evolve and deepen our ikigai.

DAY 268 • MANABIGAI AND OSHIGEAI • 学びがいと教えがい

Yu's ikigai is a combination of both *manabigai* (that which is worth learning) and *oshiegai* (that which is worth teaching). It is clear he has a love for learning, but he also enjoys applying his newfound knowledge in the classroom, acknowledging that he also learns from his students. Yu's manabigai feeds his oshiegai, which in turn feeds back into his manabigai to create, in his words, a virtuous cycle. When have you felt that teaching something helped you understand it better—or that learning something sparked a desire to share it?

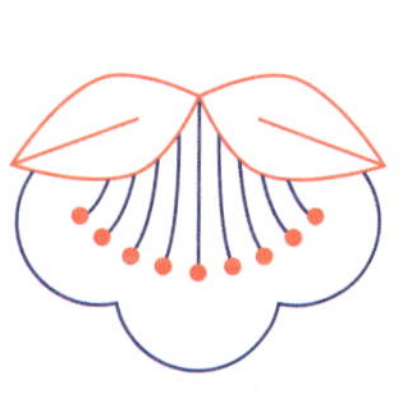
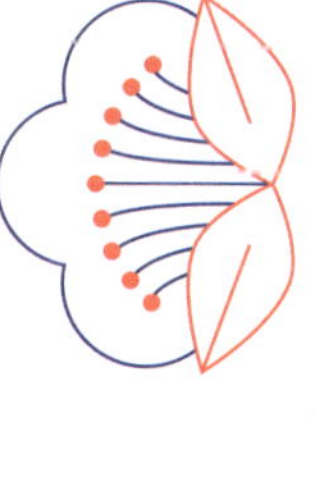

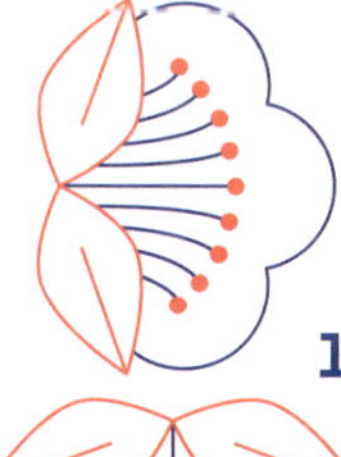
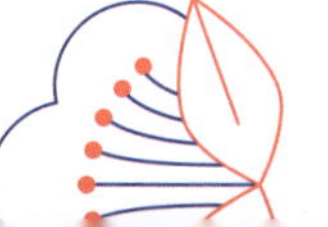

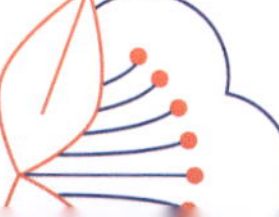

DAY 269 • SHAKUHACHI • 尺八

Kizen Oyama is a forty-year-old shakuhachi performer. *"Through performing and teaching the shakuhachi, a traditional Japanese bamboo flute, I feel a deep sense of purpose in sharing the beauty of the shakuhachi, Japanese music, and Japanese culture with others. I also find great happiness in transcending language barriers and sharing emotional connections with people worldwide through music. Having the ikigai of the shakuhachi brings me daily joy through new discoveries."* Kizen's practice shows how music can be more than art—it's a bridge. Through each note, he shares identity, history, and feeling. Ikigai flows not only from what we express, but from how others feel it.

DAY 270 • SHARING EMOTIONAL CONNECTIONS THROUGH MUSIC

Like food, music is a universal source of ikigai that brings an array of emotions to our lives, including joy, excitement, nostalgia, comfort, longing, and even sadness. As Kizen shared, music transcends language barriers and allows us to experience the wisdom, ideas, and lives of those who came before us, enriching our own lives many times over. This is perhaps felt even more deeply by those who play and teach music, especially when it involves a traditional musical instrument and style. It may be a cliché, but music does make the world go 'round. What music is your ikigai, and how do you use it to express emotion, history, or identity?

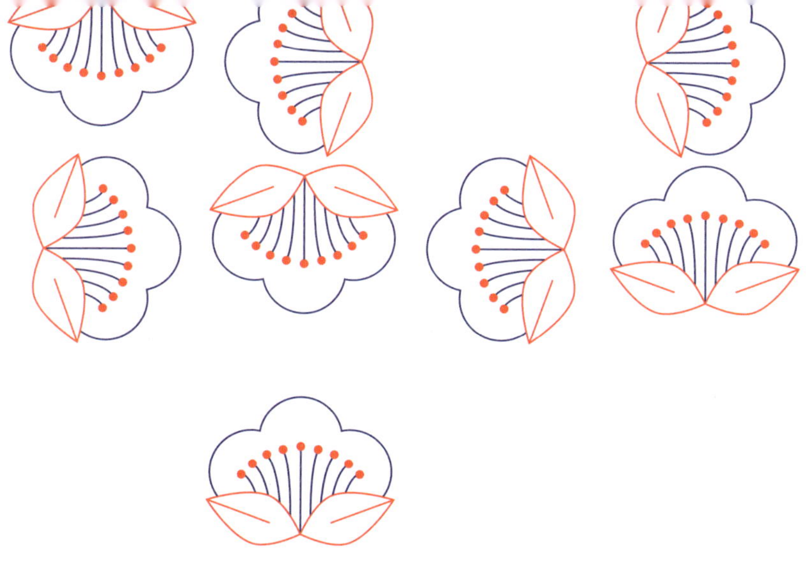

DAY 271 • FOREST BATHING RUN

Yasushiro Kotera is a forty-one-year-old associate professor and a father of four children, including triplets. *"My ikigai is to slowly run in the park near my house. After I take my children to school every morning, I take a slight detour on my way home to enjoy a slow run through the park. It's a forest bathing run, allowing me to immerse myself in nature. Without this practice, my life would feel less balanced and far more overwhelming."* Yasushiro's simple morning run reflects how natural movement can restore clarity and peace. As we step into nature, we step into ourselves—a rhythm that connects breath, body, and the present moment.

DAY 272 • EXERCISE IN NATURE

Movement in nature—whether walking, running, swimming, or simply stretching under the sky—can soothe our minds and energize our bodies. The combination of fresh air, sunlight, and natural scenery invites calm and clarity into our daily lives. This active connection with the outdoors helps us build emotional resilience while nurturing physical well-being. What activities help you feel most alive and grounded in nature?

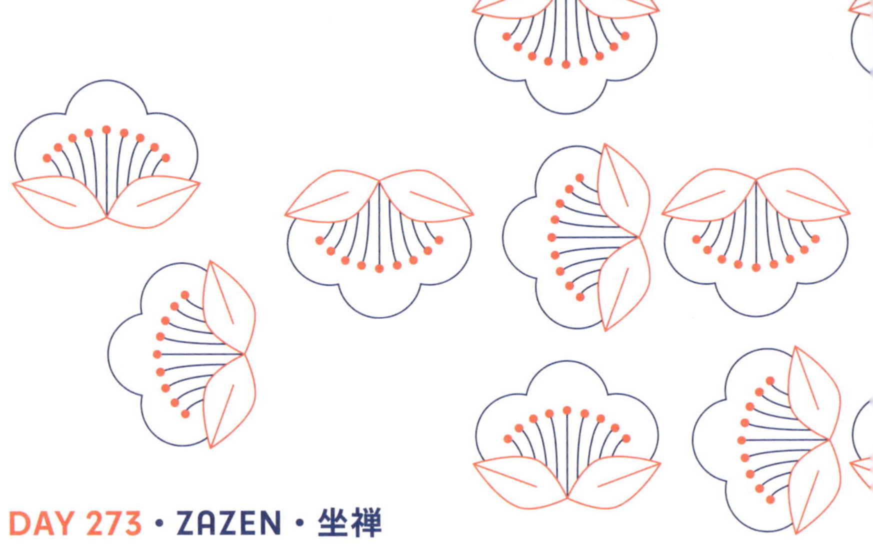

DAY 273 • ZAZEN • 坐禅

Tosei Shinabe is a forty-one-year-old Zen monk living in Kyoto, Japan. *"Zazen, seated meditation, is my vocation to pass it on to those who seek it. When I sit in zazen with someone and witness them break through a psychological barrier, I feel a deep sense of ikigai. Whenever I share this experience with someone and feel a genuine resonance with another, I'm reminded of how meaningful this work truly is, because in that moment, the world becomes a freer place for that person."* Tosei's quiet practice shows how stillness can open doorways. Even without words, presence can be a powerful guide toward clarity and transformation.

DAY 274 • HELPING OTHERS BREAK THROUGH BARRIERS

Work can most certainly be a source of ikigai, especially when it gently nudges someone beyond a barrier they didn't know they could pass. As Tosei's practice reveals, transformation doesn't always come through effort—it can arise from stillness, attention, and being fully present. Sharing space with someone as they reclaim a part of themselves is powerful, humbling, and deeply fulfilling. What quiet practices have helped you or someone you care about find a moment of clarity or breakthrough?

DAY 275 • HAPPINESS

Ikuyo Shoka is a forty-four-year-old owner of an organic kitchen restaurant in the tourist town of Inuyama in Aichi Prefecture. *"When I can make people happy or meet their expectations, I feel a rush of joy. Seeing the smiles of those I've made happy truly fills me with joy. Those smiles are my energy, my source of strength, and my ikigai! Of course, it's not just about making others happy. Knowing I've made myself happy is the most fulfilling ikigai of all."* Ikuyo reminds us that happiness is cyclical—when we lift others up, we are lifted, too. Her ikigai reflects how joy multiplies through connection and shared experience.

DAY 276 • CREATING HAPPINESS IN OTHERS

Creating happiness in others is more than a kind gesture—it's a way of life that nourishes both giver and receiver. Whether through a warm meal, a thoughtful word, or a moment of presence, simple acts have lasting impact. Ikuyo's story reminds us that joy doesn't need grandeur; even a smile exchanged in honesty can spark lasting energy. The beauty lies in reciprocity: Happiness shared becomes happiness doubled. What everyday acts of kindness or connection can help you cultivate shared joy and a deeper sense of ikigai?

DAY 277 • CONNECTIONS WITH OTHERS

Sayaka Nakano is a forty-five-year-old full-time homemaker who participates in various volunteer activities. *"My most important ikigai is undoubtedly my family, especially my children. I also find ikigai in passing down the traditions I've inherited, preserving the wisdom and customs of our predecessors for future generations. In short, connections with others seem to be my ikigai."* Sayaka's story beautifully illustrates how ikigai can be nurtured in everyday relationships. In preserving traditions and caring for others, we build lasting ties and pass on meaning. Service, like hers, begins with the simple, heartfelt ways we show up for those around us.

DAY 278 • SERVICE TO OTHERS

Being of service often begins with connection—with the people closest to us and the stories that shape us. Sayaka's commitment to family and heritage shows that service doesn't require a stage, only presence and intention. Supporting others, preserving tradition, and offering time or care can deeply enrich lives. These small acts ripple outward, strengthening bonds and community. Ikigai grows when our service reflects who we are and what we value. What traditions, relationships, or daily actions help you serve those around you with authenticity and purpose?

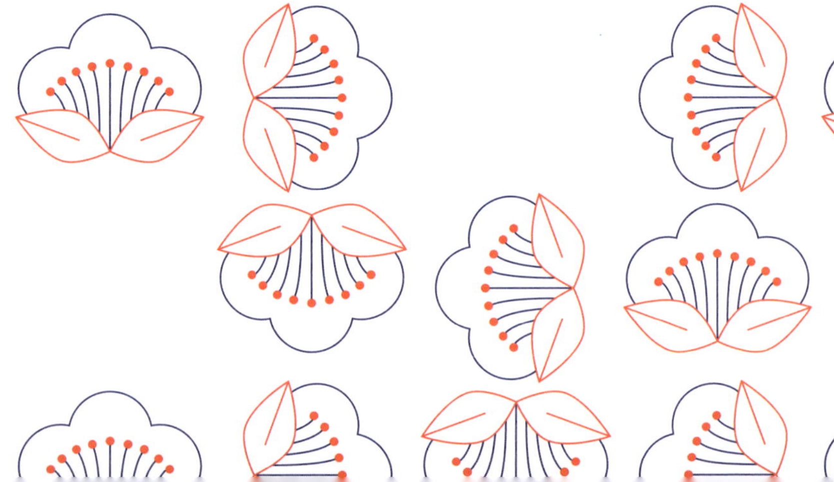

DAY 279 • RUNNING MY CAFÉ

Ayaka Kamimura is a forty-six-year-old who runs a community café in a small mountain town in Gifu Prefecture. *"My ikigai is my work of running my community café and, through it, meeting people of different ages, genders, backgrounds, and worldviews. These encounters deepen my own knowledge and perspective. I find meaning in the café functioning as a space where, even with our differences, we can build good relationships. I also feel joy when I sense that this space is helpful to someone."* Ayaka's café shows how everyday spaces can become bridges across differences. When we gather with openness and curiosity, even small interactions can spark mutual growth.

DAY 280 • DIVERSITY

Work isn't just about productivity—it's also about connection. Ayaka's café reminds us that diverse relationships strengthen our sense of purpose. Exposure to different ideas and worldviews can deepen empathy and broaden perspective. Whether we're serving, collaborating, or simply sharing space, diversity invites us to reflect, listen, and learn. When our workplaces and communities become spaces of inclusion, we create conditions for ikigai to flourish. Who can you get to know more at your workplace or in your community who is different from you?

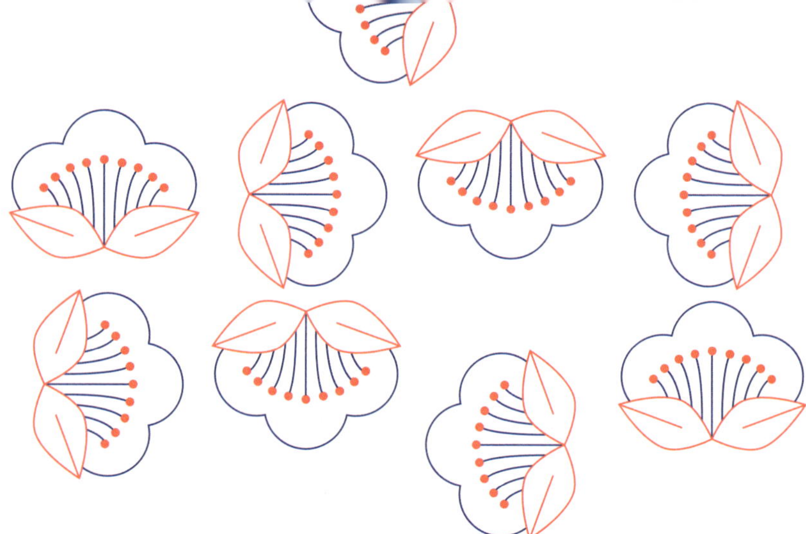

DAY 281 • CREATING A BRIGHT FUTURE

Yukako Nakata is a forty-six-year-old sales assistant with two daughters. *"My ikigai is to do all that I can now in order to create a life so that when I eventually have grandchildren, I and those around me can live in an environment of emotional, physical, and financial ease. Because I have this goal, I can endure hardship and keep going. Ikigai is something that motivates me to do my best."* As we can see in Yukako's example, enduring hardship and sacrificing for family or in the service of others can be experienced as ikigai and felt as determination.

DAY 282 • DETERMINATION

Determination often grows from a desire to serve something beyond ourselves—whether it's family, community, or a vision for the future. As Yukako shows, the strength to endure hardship is rooted in a personal mission. Sacrifice becomes meaningful when it's tethered to hope. When we focus on the long view and hold close a reason to persist, we tap into a deep and sustaining ikigai. Whether quietly or boldly, this inner drive helps us show up with resilience and purpose. In what ways does your personal mission fuel your determination through difficulty?

DAY 283 • THE OCEAN

Fujiyuki Matsumoto is a forty-seven-year-old tech worker and a part-time artist. *"My ikigai is the ocean. Whenever I need to clear my head or need to feel connected with nature, I turn to the ocean. I love visiting the beautiful and untouched coastline of the Pacific Northwest, exploring tide pools, and watching the waves. I can get lost in the fascinating designs of the fauna, creatures, and ecosystems we have in the sea."* Fujiyuki's experience shows that ikigai can arise from the quiet wonder of nature. In the rhythm of the waves and the richness of life below, we rediscover calm, curiosity, and a deeper connection to the world.

DAY 284 • RECONNECTING TO NATURE

Immersing ourselves in nature feels like reconnecting to our primal roots, where we can lose ourselves in all the awe and beauty of Mother Nature. In our chaotic world, where screen time and social media have become modern idols, the wild reminds us of the importance of letting go of the artificial and reconnecting with Earth's raw elements—to feel truly alive and part of an ecosystem that spawns all life. When was the last time you fully immersed yourself in nature? When will be the next?

DAY 285 • AIKIDO • 合気道

Mayumi Kojima is a forty-nine-year-old naturopath living in Cairns, Australia. *"I feel ikigai when I practice aikido, especially when my opponent throws me to the floor. There is something special about being repeatedly thrown and getting up again. It's almost like I am reminding myself not to give up, even when life presents hardships. Aikido also helps me become a better version of myself. It serves as a great reminder to live fully and always do my best, even in difficult times, so I have no regrets."* Through Mayumi's practice, we see how sport can carry our sense of ikigai beyond physical skill—it becomes a philosophy. Aikido transforms falling into a form of growth, and persistence into purpose.

DAY 286 • DEVELOPING RESILIENCE

Hobbies and sports can be ikigai sources that foster resilience, growth, and self-improvement. A hobby or sport can serve as a guiding force for those seeking to embrace life's challenges, strive for their best, and live with no regrets. Sports like aikido embody both experiential and philosophical elements of ikigai, teaching perseverance through the act of being thrown and rising again—mirroring the ability to overcome hardships and keep moving forward. What new hobby or sport could you practice to develop a mindset that cultivates strength, adaptability, and a deeper connection to life's purpose?

DAY 287 • MUSIC THERAPY

June Kashio is a fifty-two-year-old widow and cancer survivor. *"Music therapy helped me in my early years of grief and during cancer treatment. I took guitar and singing lessons, learning to use my breath and body as an amplifier to sing and release my emotions. As a child of the '80s, I often find myself dancing to '80s music in the kitchen—it transports me back to my youth, growing up in the UK and Japan. Having this ikigai in my life makes me smile, feel alive and energized."* June's story reminds us that ikigai can be a lifeline, helping us reconnect to joy and resilience. With each chord and chorus, she reclaims her voice and spirit.

DAY 288 • IKIGAI IS PRECARIOUS

An ikigai source such as music therapy can provide comfort while processing loss and serve as a focus when treating illness. One aspect of life that we must come to accept is that all sources of ikigai are precarious. Your ikigai is likely to vanish at some point. This is why it is important to have multiple sources of ikigai in your life, including those that can transport you back to your youth, evoke nostalgia, and, in a sense, rekindle ikigai gone by. What memories, activities, or people help you reconnect with lost parts of yourself and revive a sense of ikigai when it feels out of reach?

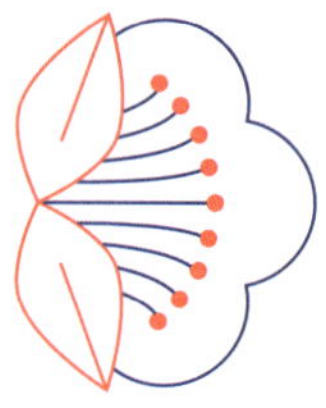
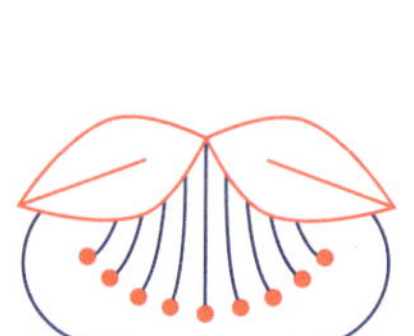
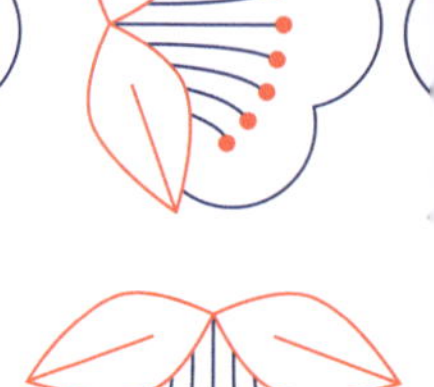
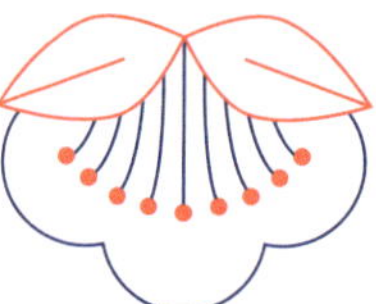

DAY 289 • IT'S WHAT GIVES MY LIFE ENERGY AND PURPOSE

Kei Tsuda is a fifty-two-year-old former corporate educator turned ikigai researcher and entrepreneur. *"My ikigai is helping others discover their own ikigai and finding fulfillment in seemingly small but meaningful moments of life. Witnessing the spark of realization in someone's eyes when they connect their values and purpose fills me with a profound sense of joy and accomplishment. It's like watching a seed take root and begin to grow—subtle but powerful."* For Kei, ikigai blooms through guiding others. It's not about grand gestures, but quiet transformations. His work reveals that purpose can emerge from helping others find theirs—reminding us that the energy we pour into others often flows back into our own lives.

DAY 290 • SEED OF PURPOSE

Kei's journey shows how ikigai is entwined with purpose—especially when that purpose lies in service. In helping others uncover what fulfills them, we reinforce our own sense of meaning. Relationships become mirrors and catalysts for growth. The impact stretches beyond the personal, shaping communities and cultures of care. If your role allows you to nurture others—whether as a mentor, friend, or teammate—you may find that the most rewarding form of ikigai is seeing someone flourish because you showed up. How might you help someone plant their seed today?

DAY 291 • MULTIPLE IKIGAI SOURCES

Masayuki Matsubara is a fifty-two-year-old father and entrepreneur. *"I have many ikigai sources. One is seeing my son every Sunday. Another is taking a walk by the river in the evening to admire nature under the sunset glow. I also play the piano and compose music for an hour every morning. These activities refresh my mind and help me relieve stress."* Matsubara's day is filled with simple yet meaningful activities that bring him joy—his personal sources of ikigai. The key isn't just the activities themselves but his proactive approach in seeking them out and his ability to be fully present as they unfold.

DAY 292 • IKIGAI ROUTINES

Masayuki's ikigai routine isn't about chasing grand ambitions; instead, it's built on small, fulfilling moments—connecting with someone he loves, appreciating nature, expressing creativity, and strengthening his body and mind. What everyday activities bring you joy and fulfillment? How might you create your own ikigai routine?

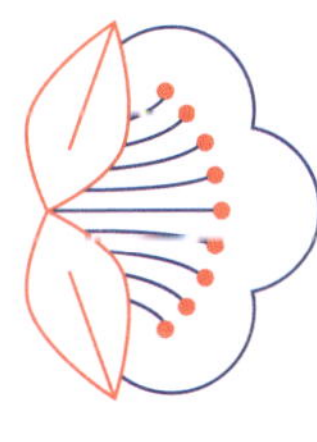

DAY 293 • APPRECIATING THE MAGNIFICENCE OF NATURE

Takehiro Tomita is a fifty-three-year-old scientist and business owner living in Australia. *"My ikigai is observing the leaves and branches at the very top of eucalyptus trees during my walks or from my home. When I think about how water absorbed by the roots travels all the way up to nourish the leaves, I am struck by the greatness of nature's mechanisms. Watching the eucalyptus leaves and branches at the very top gently sway in the wind calms my heart and fills me with an incredible sense of comfort."* Takehiro's reflection reminds us that ikigai doesn't always come from action—it can also arise from awe. In quiet observation, we reconnect to the intelligence and serenity of life itself.

DAY 294 • AN ABUNDANCE OF IKIGAI

We must be present to witness and appreciate ikigai in the world around us. You might think that observing something so ordinary, so commonplace, is not a real source of ikigai, but when you take a moment to reflect on the workings of nature, you'll find awe all around you. Unfortunately, we often miss these ikigai triggers because we are stuck in our heads or glued to a screen, rarely present enough to notice the greatness of nature's mechanisms. Take a moment today to go outside or take a walk and just breathe in the fresh air, stopping to notice the potential wonders you can see.

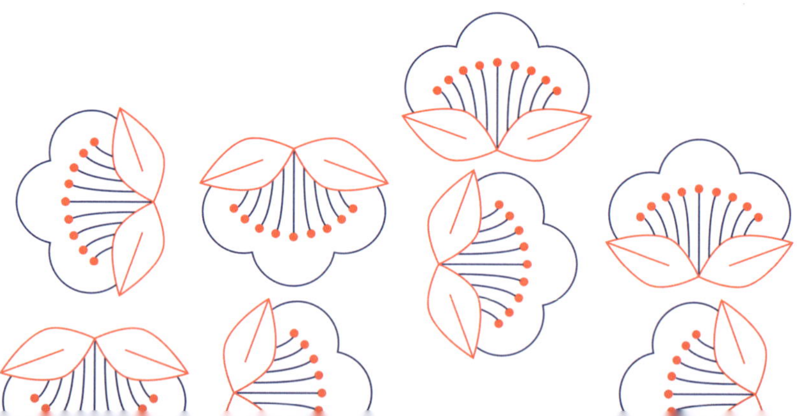

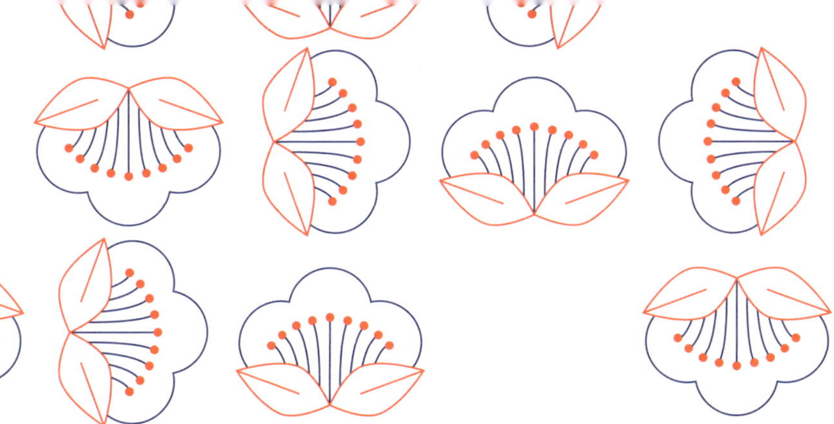

DAY 295 • MAKING CRAFTS FOR OTHERS

Kaoru Hayashi is a fifty-two-year-old mother of one and retail assistant. "*My ikigai is the time I spend creating things by hand. I love all kinds of crafts—embroidery, knitting, crocheting, and others. Occasionally, I make things as gifts for others. During those times, I enjoy thinking about what the person likes and how I can reflect their personality in the piece. I realize that while I'm making a gift for someone else, I'm also receiving a gift from them—the gift of a happy, peaceful time—and I feel truly grateful.*" Kaoru's practice shows that ikigai often lives in small acts of care. Crafting becomes a quiet dialogue between giver and receiver—one built on attention, gratitude, and love. Through creating, we connect.

DAY 296 • CREATIVE THOUGHTFULNESS

Creative thoughtfulness—deeply thinking of others and creating something for them—is a satisfying source of ikigai. It comes with creative expression, sense of purpose, and love. Consideration, energy, effort, diligence, and patience all go into creating something by hand, yet the process is a joy. As Kaoru pointed out, making something for others becomes a gift in return—a peaceful, joyful time that nourishes the giver as much as the receiver. We could call this time, when you make something for others, ikigai time.

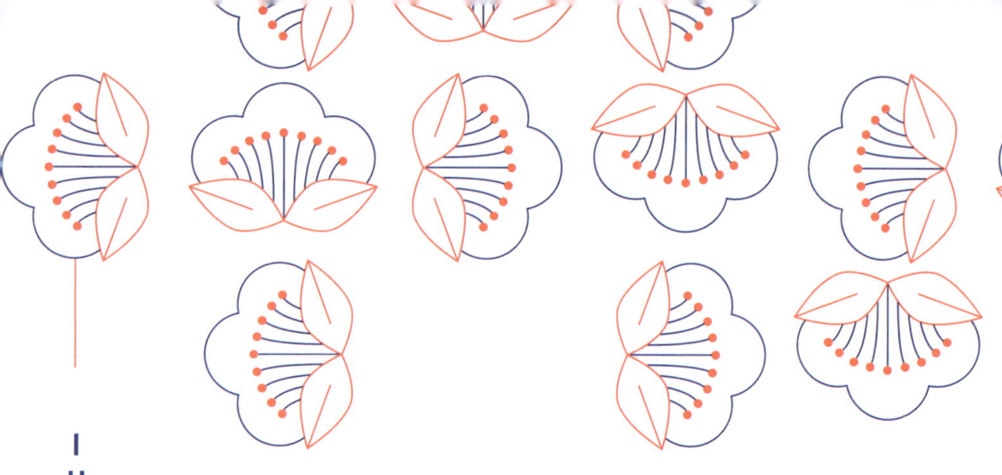

DAY 297 • JAPANESE TEA CEREMONY • 茶の湯

Akira Kishitani is a fifty-three-year-old university professor. *"My ikigai is learning Japanese tea ceremony. About once a week, I practice tea ceremony with my sensei. I really love this quiet time and the taste of both wagashi, traditional Japanese sweets, and matcha tea. Starting this year, my son will join me in learning tea ceremony, which brings even greater joy to my life."* Akira's practice of the Japanese tea ceremony shows how ikigai can be found in mindful rituals and generational connection. Through this weekly tradition, ikigai passes gently from one hand to another, steeped in love and intention.

DAY 298 • TRADITIONAL CRAFTS

Learning and practicing a traditional craft such as the Japanese tea ceremony offers many rewards: a connection between student and teacher, the preservation of cultural heritage, and the pursuit of mastery through ritual. These experiences often become even more meaningful when shared with a friend or family member. The joy of learning deepens when someone joins you on the journey, allowing for reflection, growth, and connection. What traditional craft or practice might you dedicate your time and care to? And who could you invite to walk beside you on that path?

DAY 299 • RESPECTING AND EVOLVING TRADITIONAL SYSTEMS

Naoko Mikami is a fifty-four-year-old calligrapher and cultural ambassador who shares Japanese philosophy through her art and writing. *"Perhaps my ikigai lies in respecting traditional systems while striving to evolve them. Calligraphy, bound by rules, can sometimes feel stifled, but creativity has the power to transform it, and life in general, into something far more meaningful. Another source of joy is seeing my work resonate with others. Whether it's a collector finding personal meaning or someone discovering the beauty of Japanese calligraphy for the first time, these connections inspire me to keep exploring this path."* Naoko's journey reminds us that ikigai isn't static—it flows between reverence and innovation. Creativity becomes a bridge between tradition and possibility, breathing new life into old forms while honoring their roots.

DAY 300 • CREATIVE TRANSFORMATION

Although calligraphy itself may not be Mikami's ikigai, it's the gateway to something deeper—creative expression. Whether through art, music, writing, or another imaginative craft, creativity has the power to stir something within us: awe, curiosity, serenity. For Mikami, creativity transforms the structure of tradition into something personal and meaningful. It's also about connection—when others resonate with her work, she feels inspired to continue. Creative expression allows us to offer a piece of ourselves, a unique gift that enriches both giver and receiver. What gift of ikigai can you offer others through your own creative expression?

DAY 301 • FUTURE GENERATIONS

Naoko Tomita is a fifty-four-year-old workshop facilitator and regenerative lifestyle designer. *"My ikigai lies in imagining what I can pass on to future generations. Through my regenerative house in Tateyama, I create opportunities for others to reconnect with nature, explore personal regeneration, and discover their own sense of ikigai. Having this ikigai fills my days with enthusiasm and gratitude, making me feel deeply aligned with my personal values and the vision I want to leave behind."* Naoko's ikigai shows how legacy can be cultivated through daily acts of care. Her life is a quiet blueprint for regeneration—offering others not just tools for renewal, but the inspiration to live intentionally and pass meaning forward.

DAY 302 • AN ENDURING HOPE

Naoko's ikigai extends beyond her lifetime—not just as a legacy to "leave behind" but as a gift to pass on. In her words, it is an enduring hope for humanity's ability to build a brighter future. Ikigai can be a vision of what is yet to come, a spark of inspiration that ignites something greater—something others may carry forward with their own mission. How do you envision your own ikigai extending beyond your lifetime? What values, passions, or commitments do you hope to pass on to future generations?

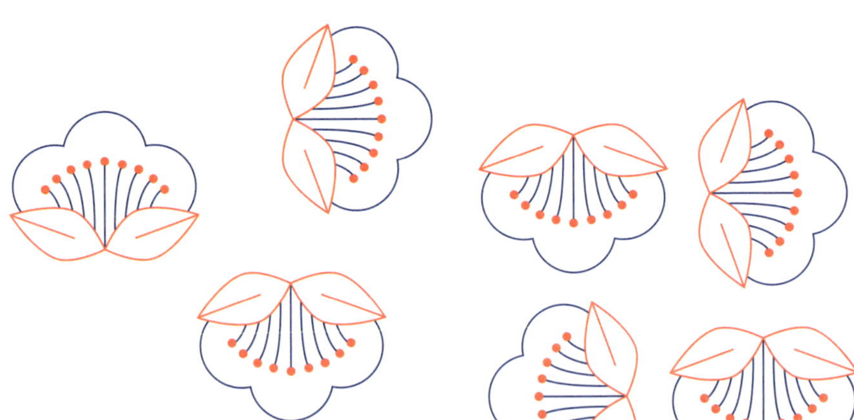

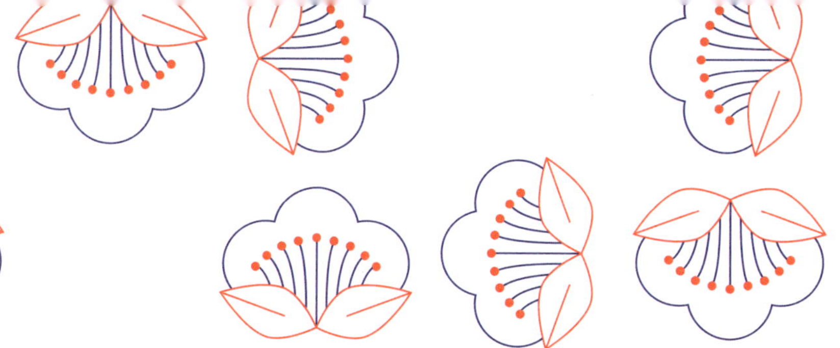

DAY 303 • FOSTERING CONNECTIONS

Kouji Miki, a fifty-six-year-old manager of a business innovation school, uses his home as a studio to train aspiring innovators. *"I have three key ikigai that drive my life: creating a sense of ikigai for others through my innovation school; sharing Zen culture with foreigners visiting Kamakura by guiding them around Japanese Zen temples; and initiating sustainable projects by connecting individuals involved in sustainability efforts. I find joy in unlocking people's creativity and fostering connections that contribute to building a better world."* Kouji's story reminds us that ikigai often flourishes where creativity meets community. Whether nurturing ideas, sharing culture, or connecting change-makers, each action reflects purposeful care. These threads weave together into the greater tapestry of a life driven by intention.

DAY 304 • PURPOSEFUL ACTIONS

Articulating one's ikigai can be challenging, but for those who tie ikigai to their professional life, it often emerges from meaningful connections and purposeful actions. As Kouji shared, he finds ikigai through his work—fostering innovation, sharing Zen culture, and supporting sustainability. Each of his sources requires clear intention, planning, and energy, much like how many people shape their own ikigai through careers, relationships, or passions that align with their values. Can you shape a new ikigai source in your professional life? What would that look like?

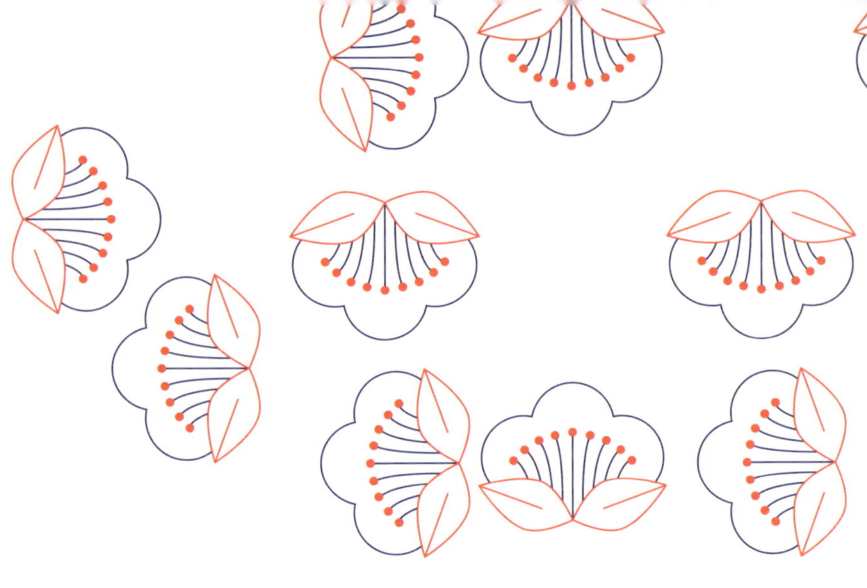

DAY 305 • INDULGING IN NATURE

Misako Yoke is a fifty-eight-year-old haiku poet and author. *"Indulging myself in nature is without a doubt my ikigai. After stressful days or weeks, going into the wilderness and reconnecting with my love of exploring rejuvenates my energy, helps me reset, and find clarity."* Nature as an ikigai source can provide something to look forward to, a place of refuge and recovery, and a source of inspiration for creative expression.

DAY 306 • NATURE'S INSPIRATION

Misako's example illustrates how a single source of ikigai has so much to offer us: energy, fulfillment, purpose in life, inspiration, and self-authenticity. Nature as an ikigai source is a gift that keeps on giving. It sparks creative expression, nourishes the spirit, and reminds us of our place in something larger. When we slow down to observe, we often find ourselves moved to create, reflect, and reimagine. In what ways does nature inspire you? What might it help you express?

DAY 307 • A LIFE FULL OF IKIGAI

Yasushi Uemura is a fifty-eight-year-old father and freelance designer. *"Reflecting on ikigai, I would say that everything in my life holds ikigai. I have always made the effort to value the things that are meaningful to me and tried to live my life accordingly. As a result, I can confidently say that my life is full of ikigai. I am fortunate to be surrounded by the things I love: my family, challenging work, good friends, and enjoyable hobbies. I feel that all of these are irreplaceable. They are my ikigai."* Yasushi's reflections reveal that when you consistently make space for what matters, ikigai becomes a way of life. It's not just what you do—it's how you see and shape your world. This sense of alignment is what we might call an "ikigai mindset."

DAY 308 • AN IKIGAI MINDSET

Living with an ikigai mindset doesn't require constantly thinking about the concept itself—it's about having the self-belief and courage to pursue what truly matters. Those who embody this mindset often live by their own rules, guided by a deep sense of purpose and self-acceptance. How can you live by your own rules to pursue the things in life that hold meaning for you?

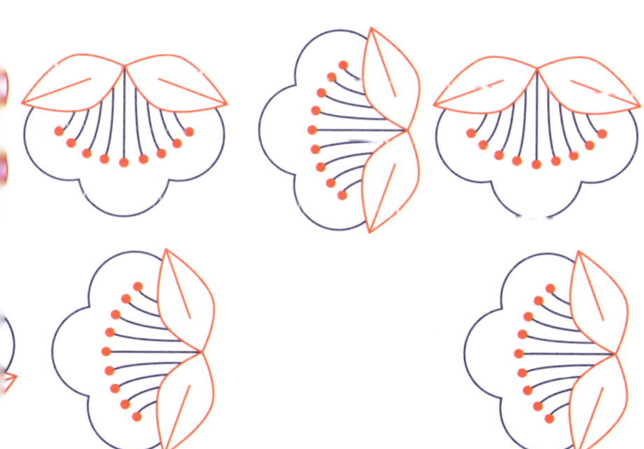

DAY 309 • A LIFE WORTH DOING

Shinji Kimura is a sixty-year-old residential construction manager. *"I don't really feel I have ikigai in my life. In my opinion ikigai is only experienced when we procreate and raise offspring. This is our strongest human instinct. As I don't have any children I don't feel I have ikigai. I do many enjoyable activities in my life, such as eating out and drinking, making leather goods, and so on. These things hold yarigai, things worth doing, for me, but I don't think they are deep enough for me to call them ikigai."* While Shinji draws a clear line between yarigai—things worth doing—and ikigai—life's deeper purpose—his reflections reveal a longing for legacy and connection. You won't always feel ikigai, and that's okay. Shinji's view reminds us that ikigai is not a constant—it's a deeply personal experience that may evolve, remain elusive, or feel absent.

DAY 310 • LIFE EXPERIENCES AND PERSONAL BELIEFS

Shinji views ikigai as the instinct to nurture life through parenting. Because he doesn't have children, he feels he doesn't experience ikigai. His perspective highlights how our sense of purpose is shaped by personal beliefs and life experiences. For others, that same drive to nurture may be expressed through creativity, relationships, or personal growth. Shinji's reflection reminds us that ikigai is not a fixed destination—it's a deeply personal journey, unique to each individual. In what ways do your personal beliefs or life experiences shape how you define ikigai—and how might your definition differ from others'?

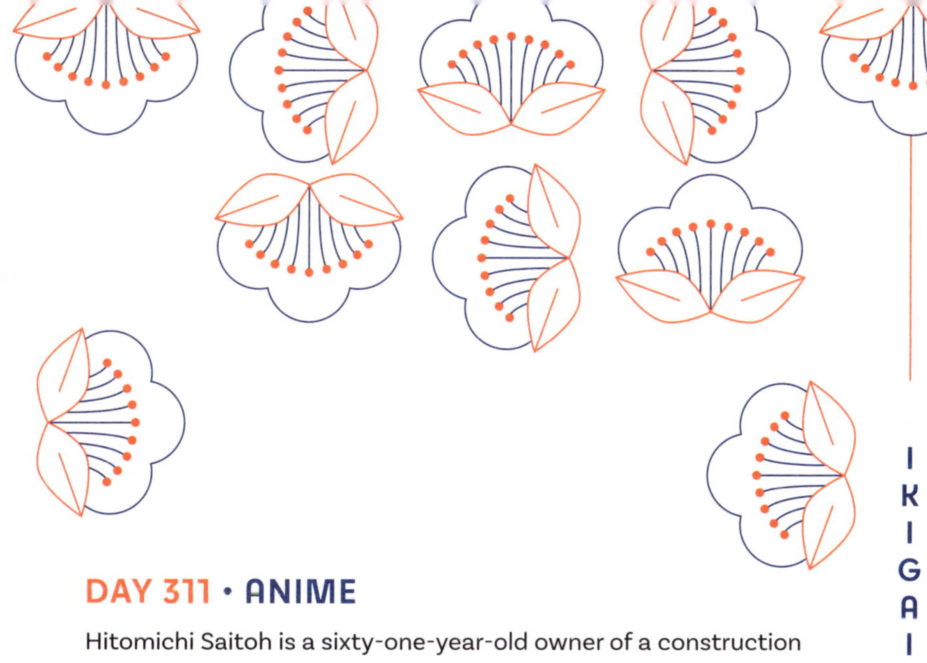

DAY 311 • ANIME

Hitomichi Saitoh is a sixty-one-year-old owner of a construction company. *"My ikigai is watching anime. I work long hours and have a lot of responsibility with my company, so when I have free time, I just want to switch off, have some time to myself to just relax, and forget about work. Watching anime makes me forget about all my responsibilities for a few hours."* For Hitomich, anime serves as a portal to rest and renewal—a source of emotional escape and inner recharge. Ikigai doesn't always have to be productive; it can simply be something that nurtures joy and presence. Time for ourselves helps us balance life's demands and reconnect us with who we are.

DAY 312 • A COPING MECHANISM

As we can see with Hitomichi, an ikigai source can offer comfort and relief in the midst of one's busy and demanding life. Having "me time" with something familiar that you enjoyed doing in your childhood can serve as a coping mechanism to help you handle all the adult responsibilities that come with work and family. What could be your ikigai coping mechanism—something relaxing that doesn't require too much effort—when life becomes overwhelming?

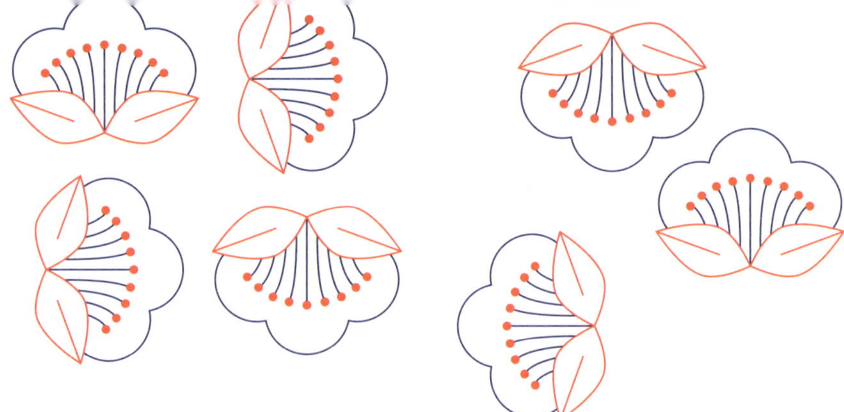

DAY 313 • MY MISSION IN LIFE

Sachiaki Takamiya is a sixty-two-year-old writer and YouTuber who promotes health and longevity. *"My main ikigai is my work, promoting health and longevity through my "Ikigai Bio-Hacking" method. I feel this is my mission in life and feel fulfilled when I write or make YouTube videos about it. I have many minor ikigais, such as exercising and having saunas, but one that stands out is speaking in English. I find great pleasure in communicating with people worldwide, which adds another dimension to my work, as I create content in English."* Sachiaki's story reflects the beauty of having both a central purpose and a constellation of smaller joys. Ikigai can be a lifelong mission, like sharing knowledge to help others live better, and it can also be found in simple pleasures that enrich that mission.

DAY 314 • MULTIPLE IKIGAIS

Ikigai isn't bound by rules. As we have explored, there are no frameworks or sweet spots. Some sources of ikigai, by their very nature, will hold greater importance or demand more of you, such as a personal mission or a role. Yet these major ikigai don't have to come at the expense of smaller ikigais. The key is learning to balance them all so you can enjoy the affirming benefits of every ikigai source. And like Sachiaki, you can even tie your main and minor ikigai together in your work or role.

DAY 315 • SMALL ACTIONS

Ken Mogi is a sixty-two-year-old neuroscientist and author who writes about ikigai. *"Ikigai is all about making these small actions into pleasurable rewarding experiences. You can start from your morning chore of taking a cup of coffee and chocolate. I personally do that every morning and then I immediately start doing some writing or reading in the morning and my day just goes on and on without resting or having an inactive period. I can do that because I'm in an almost constant state of flow."* Following Ken's advice, taking your small daily actions and turning them into pleasurable, rewarding experiences is a simple and effective way to generate more ikigai throughout your day.

DAY 316 • DOPAMINE

Ikigai and dopamine share a two-way dance. When you do something you love, dopamine—the neurotransmitter that mediates pleasure in the brain—is released, giving you a spark of joy and motivation. This burst of reward makes life feel worth living and strengthens your sense of ikigai. At the same time, having ikigai sources or activities to look forward to can trigger dopamine through anticipation. It's a virtuous loop: dopamine fuels ikigai, and ikigai invites more dopamine.

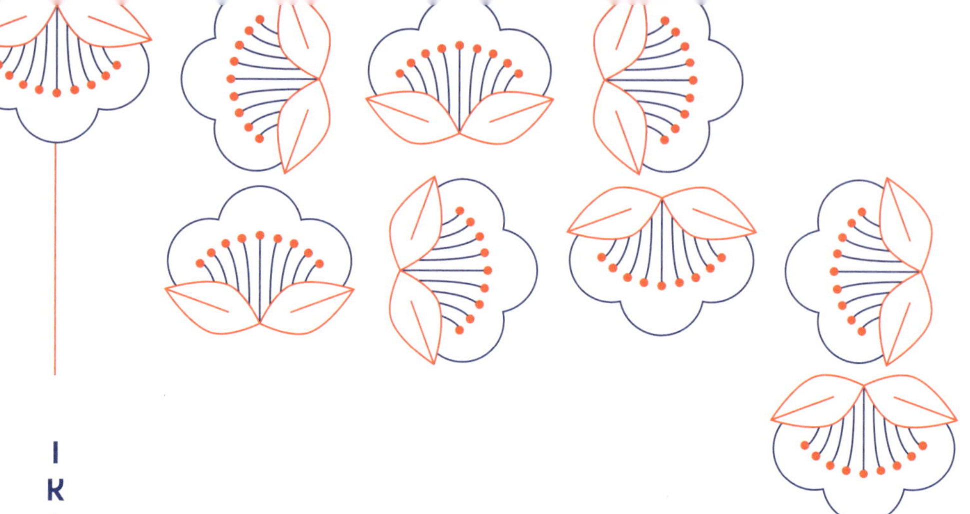

DAY 317 • FISHING AND COLLECTING ANTIQUES

Shigenobu Kato is a seventy-year-old retiree who enjoys his post-retirement life with his wife. *"My ikigai is spending time with my wife, enjoying our hobbies of fishing and antique collecting. When fishing at nearby coastlines or fishing ports, I can feel the refreshing sea breeze and experience the excitement of wondering what kind of fish I'll catch today. As for antique collecting, I find joy in imagining the artists behind the pieces I encounter, as if engaging in a conversation with people of the past. Thanks to these two hobbies, I can truly enjoy life and feel happy."* Hobbies are a common and meaningful source of ikigai, especially for retirees.

DAY 318 • IMAGINATION

Your imagination is a great way to engage your ikigai. Picturing what you're anticipating happens is a wonderful way to connect with your ikigai. For instance, if you love fishing, the excitement about the kind of fish you will catch is a great way to enhance your ikigai. The use of one's imagination might be more life-affirming than the ikigai experience itself. Imagine your ideal day—what does it look like? Are there any activities from that imagined day that you can incorporate in your day-to-day life?

DAY 319 • PEACEFUL DAYS

Yoshie Kashio is an eighty-six-year-old retired Japanese immigrant who has lived in London, UK, since 1966. *"Having lived to the age of eighty-six, I have come to see that each person's ikigai is different. Some may find it in making money through roulette, while others may dedicate themselves to caring for the elderly without expecting anything in return. It is natural for each person's ikigai to be different throughout their life. For me, at this stage, my ikigai is simply having my days pass peacefully."* Yoshie's observations offer two powerful lessons, which I've been reiterating throughout: that ikigai is something uniquely personal and that it changes over time.

DAY 320 • IKIGAI CHANGES OVER TIME

When we are young, our ikigai tends to come with a feeling of passion, as we are forward focused, looking ahead to what life will bring us. As we get older, ikigai becomes more reflective—we look back on life and appreciate the smaller, simpler things we experience as days pass. What does ikigai feel like for you at the moment? Are your ikigai sources full of zest, requiring energy, or do they calm with feelings of tranquility?

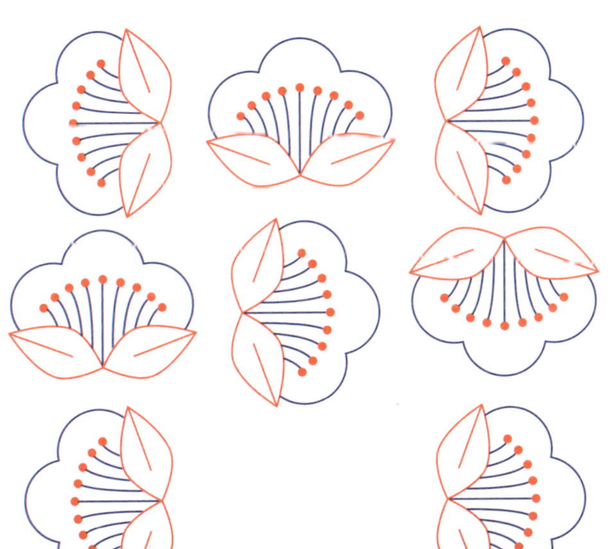

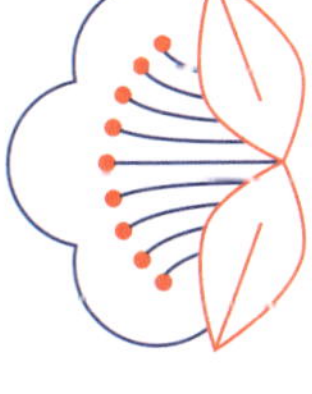

生きがいを呼び起こす

Activate Your Ikigai

DAY 321 • SMALL JOYS

There is a lot of joy to be found in the small things if we have the mind to notice them and the heart to feel them. From the morning sun's rays and the smell of coffee beans to a warm embrace with a family member or the collective laughter shared with a group of friends, we have an abundance of ikigai all around us when we can notice the small joys of life. What small joys surround you? How can you make the most of them?

DAY 322 • WHAT DO YOU WANT TO FEEL?

It's important to recognize that we are not chasing a single emotion or psychological state—namely, happiness. Instead, I encourage you to seek and embrace a spectrum of life-affirming emotions, including those that emerge from overcoming hardship and facing life's challenges—such as triumph, vindication, and redemption. Only through a blend of these emotions, feelings, and states can we experience a rich and diverse sense of ikigai-kan. Beyond happiness, what emotions do you want to feel or experience more deeply? What sources of ikigai—or meaningful challenges—might bring those emotions to life?

DAY 323 • CREATE AN IKIGAI MORNING ROUTINE

Every morning, you have a chance to start your day with some ikigai. You can create a list of dopamine-boosting activities that make you want to jump out of bed. Mine includes sunlight exposure, light exercise, coffee, a cold shower, hugs, cuddles with my cat, introspective journaling, a bit of '80s rock, a short Japanese lesson, and a little reading, all before diving into deep work. What could your morning routine be?

DAY 324 • CREATE AN IKIGAI EVENING ROUTINE

Ikigai requires reflection. Instead of binge-watching shows in the evenings, take control of your time and mind and reflect on your ikigai moments of the day. If you really want to uncover more ikigai in your life, you could commit to doing some Naikan journaling—a Japanese self-reflection practice that helps you cultivate gratitude by examining what you've received, what you've given, and the impact you've had on others. End your days with an ikigai routine of acknowledging the ikigai you experienced during the day and anticipating the ikigai you have to look forward to tomorrow.

DAY 325 • DO THINGS PROPERLY

Take care with everything you do. Each daily chore or activity is an opportunity for you to do things with diligence and care. When you complete tasks properly, you are free to move on to other activities with a clear mind, allowing you to focus on more ikigai. Remember, doing small things well leads to doing all things well. This includes your social interactions with others. Greet with intention. Speak with intention. Thank with intention.

DAY 326 • REMEMBER THE GOOD TIMES

Ikigai can be found in the joyful memories you've shared with others. Catching up with friends and laughing over days gone by can spark a deep sense of connection and meaning. Reminiscing about your happiest moments, misadventures, and even your most embarrassing stories brings those experiences back to life. Nostalgia becomes a kind of ikigai time machine—one you ride together. Reliving these memories strengthens bonds and reminds you of how much ikigai you've already lived. This week, invite a friend to reminisce with you. Notice how the memories make you feel—perhaps a little lighter, younger, and freer, if only for a moment.

DAY 327 • CREATE AN IKIGAI BUCKET LIST

Today, create a bucket list of everything you wish to accomplish. Let your imagination run wild. It can include exotic travel destinations, extreme adventures, or goals you hope to accomplish. But also consider activities that will not only make you feel alive, but also bring meaning and significance to your life. For example, instead of taking a holiday to an exotic destination, you could write down the names of all the people who have helped or positively impacted you and meet them in person to thank them. Think of all the places that journey could take you. Who would be the first person you would like to visit?

DAY 328 • RELEASE YOUR INNER CHILD

Releasing your inner child is not about being childish but about embracing playfulness when the context is appropriate.

As children, play was the one activity we eagerly sought, giving us a sense of freedom and allowing us to express our creativity. However, as we grew older, being playful took a backseat to the more "important" things in life. In this transition, we lost a part of ourselves that we were naturally wired to engage with.

From time to time, release your inner child to experience more ikigai. What is your inner child calling you to do?

DAY 329 • SPEND TIME WITH YOUR IKI-GUYS

Spend more time with your iki-guys: the people who generate the feeling of ikigai for you and the people with whom you can share your ikigai sources. Think of your life without these people in your world. There is a chance that they may leave this world before you do. Live by the Japanese proverb, "A friend is what one should hold onto." Is there a friend you have been meaning to catch up with but have been putting off? Reach out to them today.

DAY 330 • PRACTICE ROLEFULNESS

Do you remember the three fundamental behaviors of rolefulness? Exchange greetings, have conversations, and express gratitude. Today, engage in small talk with people in your community. Alternatively, have deep and meaningful conversations with family and friends. And thank people for all that they do for you. Don't skimp on the small things or what may seem trivial. Express thanks at every opportunity. Visit a local business—perhaps a café or restaurant you like to support—and practice rolefulness with the staff.

DAY 331 • SPEND TIME IN NATURE

Reconnecting with nature gives us an opportunity to reclaim hours lost to technology, social media, and other modern distractions—all of which can be beneficial at certain times and in certain doses, but which, as studies repeatedly show, do not offer the same well-being-boosting effects as being outdoors. Stepping away from these digital distractions gives us the chance to find inspiration in the awe of nature and possibly spark a personal transformation within ourselves. Plan a weekend camping or glamping trip in nature this month.

DAY 332 • MAKE IKIGAI DECISIONS

Think carefully about what you want in life, and then make ikigai decisions. This may involve making difficult choices, having an uncomfortable conversation, or giving up something now to experience more ikigai in the future. It might also mean making decisions that require effort and follow-through. You shape your future with the ikigai decisions you make today. The alternative is to make no decision at all and remain in the status quo. In your journal, answer the following question: What one decision would bring more ikigai into your life right now?

DAY 333 • LET GO

Let go of regret, perfectionism, and worry. These are burdens you place on yourself. Most of what you fear isn't real. Letting go of false beliefs and insecurities creates space for more ikigai. But how do you let go? Start by noticing what you're holding on to. Question whether those thoughts are true or helpful. Rinse and repeat when they come up again. Letting go isn't a one-time act. It's a daily practice of challenging what stifles you. What can you begin to let go of today to make room for something more meaningful?

DAY 334 • BE VULNERABLE WITH YOUR IKIGAI

Ikigai thrives when you have the courage to be vulnerable. Hiding your ikigai sources may protect you in the short term, but over time you end up living in a world of lies that only you know about. Being vulnerable frees you from these lies to explore and pursue a life of meaning. Your ikigai might not always be understood or accepted, but that's okay, because when you reveal it, you'll have already accepted it and yourself. And that's what matters most. What ikigai sources have you been hiding? Who would you like to share them with?

DAY 335 • AVOID THE HATERS

Unfortunately, we all encounter haters—people who don't want you to feel ikigai. They'll criticize what's important to you, sabotage your happiness, undermine your growth, relish your setbacks, and manipulate you by playing the victim. It's only because they lack ikigai in their own lives that they want you to feel the same. Eliminate these people from your life or avoid them as much as possible, because accommodating their behavior will definitely not make your life feel worth living. In short, don't tolerate mistreatment from anyone who doesn't support you and your ikigai.

DAY 336 • FIND YOUR PLACE TO BE

The word *ibasho*, like ikigai, has no direct translation and is used casually in daily conversations. Ibasho translates to "whereabouts; place; location," but in recent decades, the word has been used in relation to belonging and mental well-being. An ibasho can be both a physical location, such as a café or park, or a social niche or community. It is where you can connect with those who are important to you and feel you have a place in the world. Ibasho is your place of ikigai. Where is this place for you?

DAY 337 • SUPPORT AND BELIEVE IN THE IKIGAI OF OTHERS

One of the most powerful ways to uplift someone is by believing in what matters to them. It's the greatest gift you can give, to show someone that what matters to them also matters to you. When you encourage someone's ikigai, whether it's a dream, hobby, or daily ritual, you help them feel good about themselves and what they are doing. Be the person who listens with curiosity, offers reassurance without judgment, and stands by them as they pursue what gives their life meaning. Who in your life needs to hear that you believe in their ikigai? How can you support them?

DAY 338 • BELIEVE IN IKIGAI

Ikigai is something to believe in. Whether it is an injustice you'd like to correct, a cause you'd like to pursue, or a craft or hobby you'd like to excel at, it is something that encourages you to live life fully. Having something to believe in is your superpower. It widens your eyes to see that the world is a larger place, yet narrows your focus to make you feel you can contribute meaningfully to something you care about. What is a purpose-driven ikigai you have been wanting to pursue but have put on hold? Explore your thoughts on what's holding you back.

DAY 339 • VALUE YOURSELF

You are one of a kind and have something to offer others. You are worthy of a meaningful life. You are worthy of ikigai. When you accept and value yourself, you become a source of ikigai for those around you. But when you dismiss the value you bring, it can make it harder for others to connect with you, resulting in a loss of ikigai for everyone involved. You are a unique source of ikigai. Value what you bring to others and to the world. Reflect on your strengths and how you bring a little ikigai into the lives of others.

DAY 340 • FOCUS ON THE IKIGAI OF TODAY

Focus on your ikigai of today. While it's natural to look forward to the future, remember that even anticipation is felt in the present moment. Ikigai can live in the anticipation of tomorrow, but it's always felt in the present. So rather than getting lost in distant dreams or waiting for the "right time," focus on what brings you joy, purpose, or peace today—because even looking forward is something we experience right now. The Japanese saying "one day, one life" suggests that each day is as complete and significant as an entire lifetime. I don't want to be so cliché as to preach, "Live each day to the fullest," but at least try to live fully, even if only for a brief moment, and savor the ikigai that today has to offer.

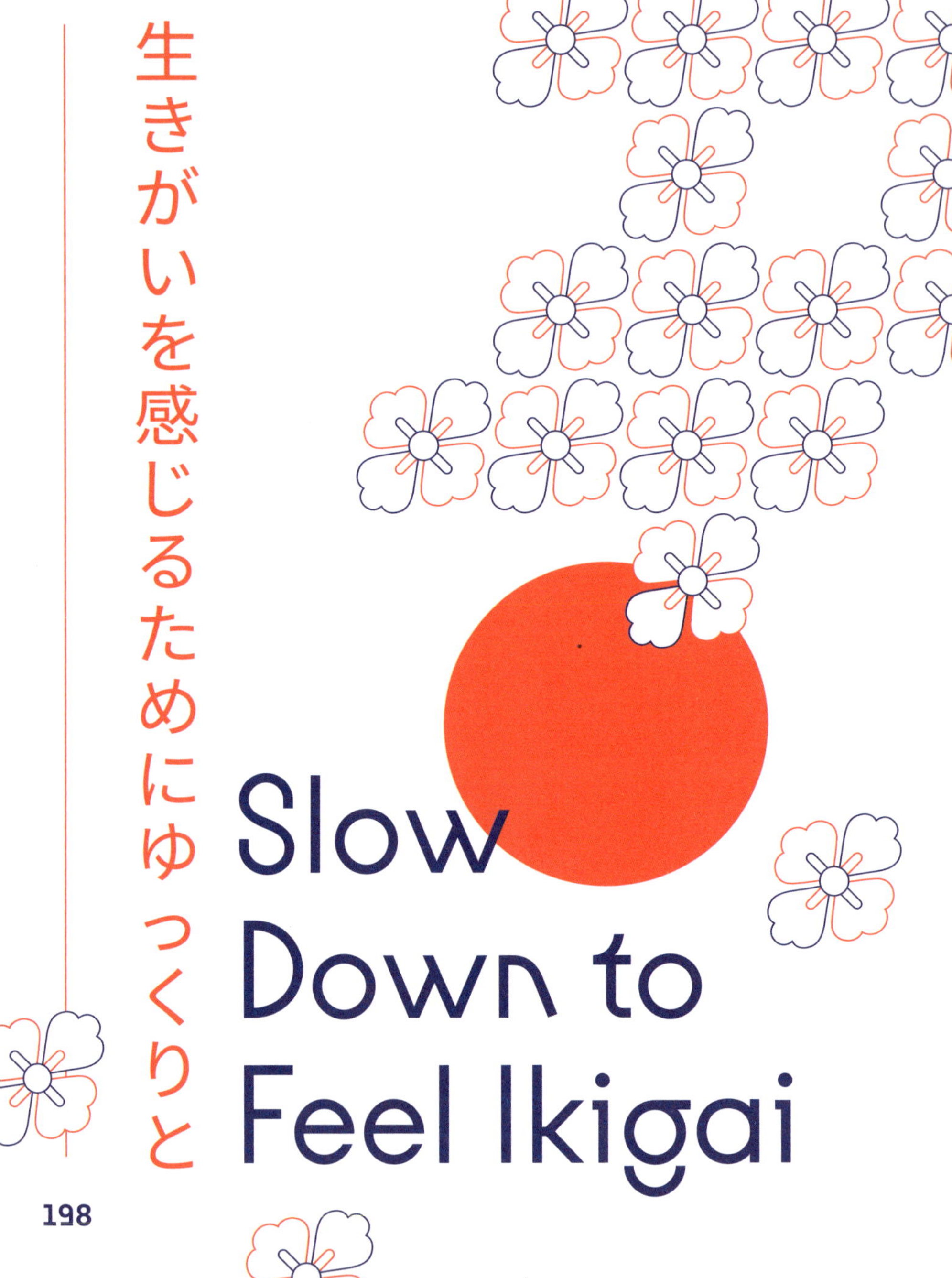

生きがいを感じるためにゆっくりと

Slow Down to Feel Ikigai

DAY 341 • ENJOY THE MOMENT

In Japanese Zen gardens, monks place boundary stones wrapped in weaved hemp at certain spots to encourage visitors to pause and appreciate a particular view. The stones cue visitors to take in the beauty in front of them and consider the design of the garden and the care and effort of its maintenance. Ikigai is like one of these boundary stones, encouraging you to pause and be present in the moment to appreciate your life and life around you. Where would you like to be more present in life? What magical moments of life are you letting pass by?

DAY 342 • SLOW DOWN TO TASTE

Do you sometimes scarf down meals without pausing to savor the flavors of each mouthful? Perhaps you do pause for the first mouthful of a delicious dessert or a new dish you're eating, but with each mouthful thereafter, your mind strays until each bite is automatic and you no longer taste the food. Take a family member, friend, or just yourself to a café or restaurant and order a dish you've never eaten before. See how slowly you can eat to fully savor the sensory pleasure—the smell, sight, texture, and taste—of each mouthful.

DAY 343 • SLOW DOWN TO SEE

Open your eyes to ikigai by pausing to focus on the beauty and awe of both the natural and artificial world. Wherever you are, you can gaze at something you've never truly seen before: the formation of clouds in the sky, the grain of a wooden table, or the architecture of the building you're in. Stop and focus your eyes on an object you've never really given your attention to. What do you see? What do you feel? What thoughts come to mind? Stay off your phone and look around—there is a world of ikigai to see.

DAY 344 • SLOW DOWN TO SMELL

Stop and smell more than just the roses. Slow down to smell the morning air. Slow down to smell your morning coffee. Slow down to smell the magic of bread turning to toast. Life's daily aromas are ikigai for your nose. Treat yourself to flowers, incense, or scented candles, and create a bouquet of fragrances for your nose to enjoy.

DAY 345 • SLOW DOWN TO LISTEN

Pause right now and listen intently. What do you hear? Perhaps it's the tweets of birds outside, the barking of a dog, or the sound of rain. If you're in a café, it might be the familiar chatter of staff and customers, the clinking of cutlery and tableware. Close your eyes for a moment and listen. Allow your ears to attune to noises you find appealing. Where do these sounds take you? What images or feelings do they conjure up? And of course, to hear a little more ikigai, you can always listen to your favorite music.

DAY 346 • SLOW DOWN TO TOUCH

We are blessed with hands. Through touch, we connect to the world and to one another. Touch grounds us in the present moment. The warmth of a cup of tea, the texture of a handmade object, the softness of another person's hand—all of these can spark small moments of ikigai. A gentle touch can often express care, comfort, and love more deeply than words. What object or surface could you explore today with mindful touch to reconnect with the present?

DAY 347 • SLOW DOWN TO BREATHE

Give your body a moment to reset. A deep breath is a moment of ikigai for your body, mind, and well-being. Every breath you take is another moment lived. Rather than letting your breaths be shallow and wasted, let them flow like the waves of a gentle tide. When you find yourself anxious or flustered, stop to breathe. Breathe in with the word *iki*—which also means "breath"—and exhale with *gai*, a word that can mean "effort," "effect," or even "outside." Breathe in with iki. Breathe out with gai. Begin and end each day with ten life-producing, life-affirming breaths of iki-gai.

DAY 348 • SLOW DOWN TO THINK

Most of the time, your mind is bouncing from one thought to another. Slow down to interrupt the flow of automatic thinking. When negative or anxious thoughts arise, pause and question them. When positive thoughts appear, take a moment to notice where they come from. Ikigai gives you focus. When you concentrate on what truly matters, your thoughts begin to settle. Slow your mind enough to be present—to reflect on the memories, people, places, and plans that bring you ikigai. What thought today is worth slowing down for?

DAY 349 • SLOW DOWN TO CONNECT

When was the last time you gave someone your full attention? Have you expressed your feelings to someone you appreciate or love in the past few days? Slow down to connect with others. Take time out of your day to reach out to a few people you care about and connect with them. It could be through a heartwarming text, a quick phone call, or a simple hug. These small gestures create space for ikigai to grow from your relationships. Who do you feel like reaching out to now?

DAY 350 • SLOW DOWN TO CHOOSE

Throughout the day, more often than not, our actions are driven by urges or impulses. But making life-affirming choices—what to drink, what to eat, what to watch, what to read, what to smell, who and what to speak and listen to, and what to give your attention to—is what cultivates ikigai. You get to decide, but you must be present in order to make choices that foster ikigai. What would bring you some ikigai right now?

生きがいを与える

Return Ikigai to Others

DAY 351 • GIVE BACK SOME IKIGAI

Consider all the ikigai others have given you over the years—from family and friends who have supported you, to those who have taught you or offered opportunities to help you earn a living. You have received an abundance of ikigai from others throughout your life. Return a little of that ikigai through thoughtful acts of kindness and expressions of gratitude. Who is the first person who comes to mind that you'd like to return some ikigai to?

DAY 352 • RETURN IKIGAI TO YOUR PARENTS

Don't wait for Mother's Day or Father's Day to express gratitude to your parents or parental figures. Return ikigai to them today with a phone call or an invitation for coffee or a meal. Surprise them with an unexpected visit. If your parents or parental figures are no longer with you, honor their memory by taking time to reflect on who they were and what they meant to you. Send them a prayer, write them a letter, or journal the fond memories you have of them.

DAY 353 • GIFT YOUR CHILDREN IKIGAI

Your children will grow up fast. Give them your full attention when they have something to tell you. Play with them. Hug them. Show them love. Tell them they make you proud—for no particular reason. And if you don't have children of your own, offer ikigai to a child you know. It could be your niece, nephew, or the child of a friend. Alternatively, you might offer your time or resources to an organization that helps children. Or perhaps your deepest bond is with a beloved pet you consider your child. They, too, thrive on your presence, affection, and care.

DAY 354 • SUPPORT THE IKIGAI OF YOUR SIBLINGS

If you have a sibling—or someone you consider to be like a sibling—support their ikigai. Whether it's a creative hobby, a professional dream, or a personal passion, show genuine interest in what lights them up. Celebrate their efforts, listen when they need to talk, and encourage them when they feel uncertain. My brother does this for me, and I'll always be grateful for it. Sometimes, the simple act of believing in someone can keep their ikigai alive. You don't need to have all the answers; just being present and supportive can make all the difference.

DAY 355 • THANK YOUR MENTORS

Much of the knowledge you now carry has been shaped by others—teachers, mentors, guides, and even those who taught you through example or experience. Think of someone who helped you grow, whether in a classroom, a workplace, a community, or simply through a moment of wisdom. A message of appreciation could mean the world to them, especially if you share how they influenced your journey. In honoring their impact, you reconnect with a source of ikigai: the joy of learning, growing, and being shaped by connection.

DAY 356 • SPEND TIME WITH YOUR FRIENDS

Friendship is a strong source of ikigai. Friends are the people we choose to spend our time with, the people in our lives who have given us our best times and who have been there for us when times have been tough. Yet life can get in the way, and we can let some friendships slip. One of life's most common regrets is not spending enough time with the people who matter to us. What's a friendship you know you should rekindle? Who should you call today?

DAY 357 • WORK AS A FORM OF IKIGAI

Work can be a powerful source of ikigai. Whether you're employed, self-employed, freelancing, or exploring new paths, your efforts can offer connection, meaning, and a chance to uplift others. Even if your relationship with work has been complex, your values and creativity can still guide how you contribute to the world. How might you bring more care, curiosity, or compassion into what you do today—not just for yourself, but for those around you? And if you're between roles, consider how your experiences have shaped your perspective, and what kind of work—or purpose—might allow you to share your ikigai with others moving forward.

DAY 358 • HONOR IKIGAI IN TIMES OF ILLNESS

Illness can be a tender chapter in someone's life—one that calls for presence, empathy, and care. If you know someone who is navigating sickness or healing, consider reaching out with kindness. A message, a shared memory, or simply your quiet companionship can offer comfort. Ask how you might support what still brings them joy, meaning, or peace. Whether it's a favorite book, a walk in the sun, or a moment of laughter, these small acts can help nurture their ikigai—and remind them they are not alone.

DAY 359 • GIVE A STRANGER AN IKIGAI HELPING HAND

The next time you see a stranger in need of a helping hand, offer it to them. We never know the burdens others carry or how close they are to falling apart. Help a stranger pay for a bill if they are short. Offer directions to someone who looks lost. Ask someone if they need help if they look distressed. A small act of kindness can go a long way. Pay your ikigai forward and make a stranger's day a little easier.

DAY 360 • GIVE BACK TO NATURE

Everything you have ever come into contact with has come from this planet—more specifically, from the workings and wonders of Mother Nature. As I mentioned in the introduction to this book, you won the jackpot in the evolutionary lottery and live each day in comfort thanks to the seemingly endless resources of nature. But nature is not an infinite resource. One way to feel a sense of ikigai and connect meaningfully to the lives of others (both living and yet-to-be-born) is to make efforts to ensure that nature thrives. How you do this is up to you.

生きがい日記

Continue Your Ikigai Journaling

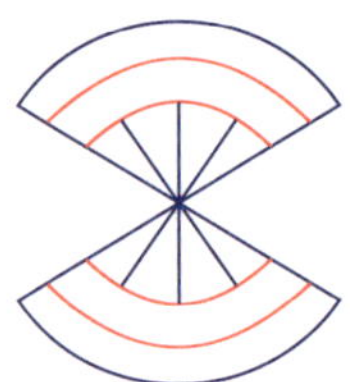

DAY 361 • KEEP JOURNALING

As we come to the end of our ikigai journey together, if there's one enduring suggestion I have, it's this: continue journaling daily—especially by hand. Ikigai requires that you know yourself, and one of the most powerful ways to deepen that self-understanding is through introspective writing. Journaling slows you down, invites reflection, and helps you notice the subtle shifts in your thoughts, feelings, and values. What has journaling revealed about your ikigai that you didn't expect? And how might your journaling continue to support your ikigai in the days ahead?

DAY 362 • CREATE A JOURNALING SPACE

Create a space for yourself to journal. You can take it a step further and create a mood. Use LED or real candles for soft lighting. Play calming ambient music to help you ease into a reflective state. Prepare a cup of herbal tea to relax and settle your mind. You might even light incense or a scented candle if that works for you. Make journaling a ritual by creating an environment that supports flow. Let journaling become a new source of ikigai in your life.

DAY 363 • FREE YOURSELF TO WRITE

I didn't journal for decades, even though I knew it would be one of the best practices I could cultivate for myself. My handwriting is terrible. My spelling is poor. My punctuation is average. I let my feelings about these things stop me from journaling. Please don't make the same mistake. Journaling is something you do for yourself. Free yourself to write. It's what you write that matters—not how well you write or how presentable your handwriting is. Journaling is something you'll come to enjoy, and its benefits can be life-changing.

DAY 364 • WRITE WITH SELF-HONESTY

When it comes to ikigai journaling, write with honesty. Write what is true for you. Let your thoughts and feelings fill the page. The purpose of ikigai journaling is to help you understand yourself and what matters to you. And to truly understand yourself, you must be honest in what you write. This is an opportunity to be selfish—to let out what you need or want to express. Release your negative emotions if you're feeling them. Write freely about your dreams and desires. Journaling is your private sanctuary for expressing your most honest thoughts and feelings.

DAY 365 • WHAT DO YOU WANT TO BE DOING?

On our last day together, I'd like to leave you with several questions. If you weren't reading this book right now, what would you like to be doing? What activity would you most like to be fully engaged in? Where would you like to be? And who would you like to be with? What role would you want to be pursuing? How do you want to use this life that has been given to you? If you can answer these questions confidently without much thought, then you are on the ikigai path.

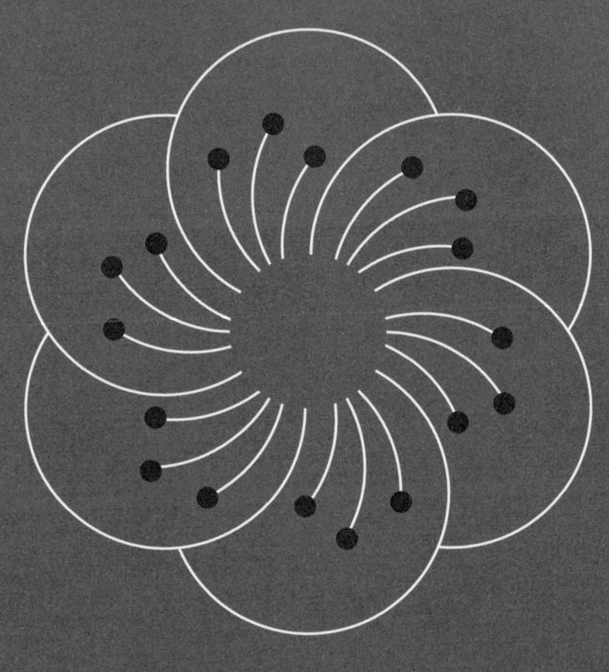

Conclusion

Making Life Worth Living

Thank you for spending this year of ikigai with me. I hope these pages have helped you uncover glimpses of your own ikigai and perhaps answered some of the questions you've carried. More than that, I hope they've inspired you to slow down, notice the small joys that make life meaningful, and cherish the people, roles, and activities that bring vitality to your days.

Remember, ikigai is not a destination—it's a companion. It will shift, evolve, and grow alongside you. It may arrive quietly, in fleeting moments, or boldly, through life-changing experiences. It shows you what matters most, and the more you nurture it, the more fulfilling your life becomes. You may have many sources of ikigai—some central, others subtle—or you may feel as if you haven't found yours yet. That's okay.

Ikigai is deeply personal. Each journey is unique, shaped by your values, your perspective, and your definition of meaning. Some, like Shinji (page 182), may feel they've yet to discover their ikigai because their idea of a purposeful life is still forming. If you feel the same, know that you're not alone. This is an ongoing journey—one of exploration, reflection, and growth. Along the way, appreciate the little things that make your life special and uniquely yours.

As you move forward with this renewed perspective, remember to pause. Make space to notice the ikigai that surrounds you. It often appears in unexpected places—during quiet mornings, in shared laughter, or even in times of challenge. But to recognize it, you must be present. You must honor it with your attention and time. Let ikigai guide you toward a life that feels deeply worth living.

Even when life feels uncertain or heavy, ikigai can be a quiet anchor. It doesn't demand perfection or grand achievements. It asks only that you pay attention—to what lights you up, what brings you peace, and what makes you feel alive. Sometimes it's a conversation, a walk, a song, a moment of stillness. Sometimes it's the courage to begin again.

So keep listening. Keep noticing. Keep honoring the things that matter to you, even if no one else sees them. Your ikigai doesn't need to be understood by others—it only needs to be felt by you.

Most of all, remember that ikigai lives within you. It's something you can express, create, and share. You can be a source of ikigai for others—through your kindness, your creativity, your presence. Let your life be a reflection of what brings you joy and meaning, and in doing so, you'll inspire others to seek their own.

And when you share it—through your work, your presence, your care—you become part of something larger. You become a spark in someone else's journey. You become a reminder that life, even in its quietest corners, is worth living.

Thank you for walking this path. May your days ahead be filled with meaning, connection, and the gentle joy of being fully alive.

Ikigai—a simple, two-syllable word with no direct translation—comes from a culture rich in wisdom and nuance. It is a gift from Japan, one that invites us to live with intention, connection, and grace. May you carry it forward with reverence and curiosity.

And as this year closes, may you continue to ask: *What makes life worth living today?* Let that question be your compass. Let it lead you toward more joy, more depth, and more days filled with meaning.

Here's to your continued journey of ikigai—may your life be vibrant, surprising, and beautifully yours.

List of Quotees

A special thanks to everyone who shared their ikigai with me.

Misaki Endo
Jun Hayashi
Kaoru Hayashi
Minako Horaguchi
Miyuki Imaeda
Fuka Itō
Shiori Jonokuchi
Ayaka Kamimura
Yu Kanazawa
June Kashio
Yoshie Kashio
Daiki Kato
Kana Kato
Kanta Kato
Genki Kato
Shigenobu Kato
Shinji Kimura
Akira Kishitani
Mayumi Kojima
Shintaro Kono
Yasushiro Kotora
Masayuki Matsubara
Maya Matsui
Fujiyuki Matsumoto
Ai Nakamura
Naoko Mikami
Kouji Miki
Ken Mogi
Chiharu Nakayama
Sayaka Nakano
Yukako Nakata
Tamaki Nishimura
Kizen Oyama
Reina Sano
Hitomichi Saitoh
Rino Sekijima
Kako Shimonishi
Tosei Shinabe
Ikuyo Shoka
Momo Suzuki
Sachiaki Takamiya
Naoko Tomita
Takehiro Tomita
Kei Tsuda
Andriana Ubunuki-Kalfa
Yasushi Uemura
Ayumi Umeda
Keiko Yamada
Misako Yoke

References

Buchanan, Daniel Crump, comp. and trans. *One Hundred Famous Haiku*. Tokyo; San Francisco: Japan Publications, 1973, 31, 40, 97. Accessed August 2025. www.thehaikufoundation.org/omeka/items/show/4390.

Blyth, Reginald Horace. *Haiku*. Tokyo: Hokuseido Press, 1981, 202. www.google.com.au/books/edition/_/iiMlJY--UP4C?hl=en&gbpv=1

Csikszentmihalyi, Mihaly, and Isabella Selega Csikszentmihalyi, eds. *Optimal Experience: Psychological Studies of Flow in Consciousness*. Cambridge: Cambridge University Press, 2000.

Fido, Dean, et al. "English Translation and Validation of the Ikigai-9 in a UK Sample: A Brief Report." *International Journal of Mental Health and Addiction*, 2019. doi.org/10.1007/s11469-019-00150-w.

Galton, Francis. "Measurement of Character." *Fortnightly Review* 36 (1884): 179–185.

General Incorporated Foundation for the Development of Health and Ikigai, and Tetsuo Tsuji, eds. *Toward a New Stage in the Era of the 100-Year Life: Building Health, Social Participation, and Ikigai through Human Connection*. Tokyo: General Incorporated Foundation for the Development of Health and Ikigai, 2019, 34.

Goldberg, Lewis R. "Language and Individual Differences: The Search for Universals in Personality Lexicons." In *Review of Personality and Social Psychology, Vol. 2*, edited by L. Wheeler, 141–65. Beverly Hills, CA: Sage, 1981.

Google Trends. "ikigai - Google Trends." Accessed August 12, 2025. trends.google.com/trends/explore?date=all&q=ikigai&hl=en-GB

Imai, Masaaki. 1986. *Kaizen: The Key to Japan's Competitive Success.* New York: McGraw-Hill, 1986.

Kamiya, Mieko. *Ikigai ni tsuite.* Tōkyō: Misuzu Shobō, 2004.

Kato, D., and M. Suzuki. "Rolefulness and Interpersonal Relationships." In *Interpersonal Relationships,* edited by Martha Peaslee Levine. London: IntechOpen, 2020. doi.org/10.5772/intechopen.95396.

Kemp, Nick, host. "Rock Star Neuroscientist, Ken Mogi's 5 Pillars of Ikigai." *The Ikigai Podcast,* season 1, episode 6. Ikigai Tribe. January 19, 2020. ikigaitribe.com/podcasts/podcast06/.

Kono, Shintaro. "Theorizing Linkages between Ikigai (Life Worthiness) and Leisure among Japanese University Students: A Mixed Methods Approach." PhD diss., University of Alberta, 2018.

Plevin, Julia. "From Haiku to Shinrin-Yoku: A Brief History of Forest Bathing." *Forest History Today,* Spring/Fall 2018. foresthistory.org/wp-content/uploads/2019/06/3-Plevin_Forest_Bathing.pdf

Sony Life Insurance Co., Ltd. *Ikigai Survey Report,* May 19, 2025, 3. www.sonylife.co.jp/company/news/2025/files/250519_project.pdf

Synnott, Mark. "Exclusive: Alex Honnold Completes the Most Dangerous Free-Solo Ascent Ever." *National Geographic,* October 3, 2018. www.nationalgeographic.com/adventure/article/most-dangerous-free-solo-climb-yosemite-national-park-el-capitan.

Acknowledgments

There are many people to thank for the realization of this book. I would like to begin with acknowledging and thanking the people of Japan, from my family and close friends to total strangers who have changed my life and shared with me their beautiful culture.

This book is the result of many conversations with Japanese friends and acquaintances, quiet reflective moments held in Japan, and the accumulation of insights from several years of study and research on the ikigai concept.

Special thanks goes to Shinji Kimura and Daiki Kato for the many hours you freely gave to me to help bring this ikigai project to life.

To my friends Hitomich Saitoh, Yasushi Uemura, Masayuki Matsubara, Makoto Furuya, Kei Tsuda, and Ken Mogi, your friendship over the years has taught me many valuable lessons about ikigai.

To my brother, Jeremy, thanks for the encouragement, bro.

I would also like to thank the members of my Ikigai Tribe community for their encouragement and support. You make up my ibasho.

Gratitude goes to the publishing team at Quarto, especially Erin Canning, Ismita Hussain, and Keyla Pizarro-Hernández.

For the referral of a lifetime, thanks go to Kasia.

And last but not least, to my wife and son — thank you for your constant love and support throughout the writing of this book and in all my ikigai pursuits.

About the Author

Nicholas Kemp is a keynote speaker, ikigai coach, and author of several books, including *Ikigai-kan: Feel a Life Worth Living* and *Rolefulness: A Guide to Purposeful Living*. He holds a Diploma of Positive Psychology and is the founder and head coach of Ikigai Tribe—a community of educators, coaches, and trainers who serve their communities using the ikigai concept. Nick's ikigai is to bring people to Japan and introduce them to Japanese culture through activities that embody ikigai during his retreat study trips and workshops.

First published in 2026 by Rock Point, an imprint of The Quarto Group,
135 West 36th Street, 13th Floor, New York, NY 10018, USA
(212) 779-4972 www.Quarto.com

EEA Representation, WTS Tax d.o.o.,
Žanova ulica 3, 4000 Kranj, Slovenia.
www.wts-tax.si

10 9 8 7 6 5 4 3 2 1

ISBN: 978-1-57715-548-5

Digital edition published in 2026
EISBN: 978-0-7603-9853-1

Library of Congress Cataloging-in-Publication Data available upon request.

Group Publisher: Rage Kindelsperger
Editorial Director: Erin Canning
Creative Director: Laura Drew
Managing Editor: Cara Donaldson
Editor: Keyla Pizarro-Hernández
Art Director: Beth Middleworth
Cover and Interior Design: Silvia Virgillo • puntuale

Printed in Huizhou City, Guangdong, China TT122025